Haiti

Haiti

by Jean F. Blashfield

Enchantment of the World
Second Series

Children's Press®

A Division of Scholastic Inc.

New York   Toronto   London   Auckland   Sydney
Mexico City   New Delhi   Hong Kong
Danbury, Connecticut

Frontispiece: Lake Saumâtre

Consultant: Laurent Dubois, Department of History, Michigan State University,
Lansing, Michigan

Please note: All statistics are as up-to-date as possible at the time of publication.

Book production by Herman Adler

Library of Congress Cataloging-in-Publication Data

Blashfield, Jean F.
  Haiti / by Jean F. Blashfield.
    p. cm.—(Enchantment of the world. Second series)
  Includes bibliographical references and index.
  ISBN-13: 978-0-516-25949-9
  ISBN-10: 0-516-25949-0
  1. Haiti—Juvenile literature. I. Title. II. Series.
  F1915.2.B55 2007
  972.94—dc22   2006036853

J
972.94
BLAS

Haiti

Cover photo:
Haitian woman

Contents

A mountain farm

A young girl

CHAPTER
ONE

Spirit and
Strength

8

VIVID BLUE WATERS LAPPING AGAINST BEACHES. Mountains slicing into the sky. Coral reefs teeming with fish. Brilliant birds that amaze the onlooker. Music that springs from the heart of a vibrant people. Mystery that cloaks the Vodou religion (often called "Voodoo" in the United States). The first nation founded by a slave revolt. Haiti is all of this, and much, much more.

Opposite: **Haiti is the most mountainous nation in the Caribbean.**

Narrow beaches line the shore near Cap-Haïtien.

A Woman Ruler

On Hispaniola, early Spanish explorers encountered an important Taino ruler named Anacaona. Anacaona, whose name means "Golden Flower," was famed among the Taino Indians for her dance, poetry, and songs. The Spanish treated the Indians badly from the time they first arrived on Hispaniola, and Anacaona resisted them. In 1503, the Spanish killed many of her people, and they arrested and hanged Anacaona.

Since it became independent in 1804, Haiti has been a troubled land. It has struggled with poverty, foreign intervention, and political instability. Wyclef Jean, a musician who was born in Haiti and now lives in the United States, encourages his fellow Haitians to change their nation. He says, "Now the whole country needs to reach deep into the spirit and strength that is part of our heritage." That spirit and strength are gifts of Haiti's turbulent history.

This carved head was made by the Taino. They lived throughout the Caribbean.

A Caribbean Land

Haiti is located on a large island on the northern edge of the Caribbean Sea, an arm of the Atlantic Ocean that lies between North America and South America. Haiti shares the island, which is called Hispaniola, with the Dominican Republic, another nation.

Explorer Christopher Columbus called the island La Isla Española, meaning "The Spanish Isle," when he landed there in 1492. Over time, that name became *Hispaniola*. Columbus called the people he met on the island "Indians," because he thought he had landed in the East Indies, the part of Asia where he was heading. The indigenous, or

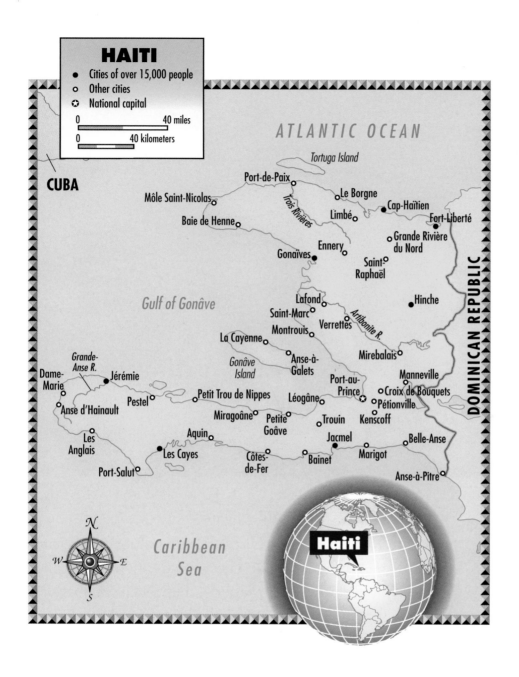

native, people of Hispaniola are usually called Taino. One name the Taino used for their land was *Ayiti*, meaning "Land of Mountains." Ayiti eventually became *Haiti*.

Haitian slaves defeated the French in the only successful slave rebellion in history.

Free and Independent

In the late 1600s, the part of Hispaniola that ultimately became Haiti fell under French rule. The French colony was called Saint-Domingue. The colony brought the French great wealth, especially through the labor of black slaves from Africa.

In the 1790s, slaves in Saint-Domingue rose up and forced the French to abolish slavery in their colonies. A few years later, French leader Napoléon Bonaparte tried to reestablish slavery. The people of Saint-Domingue fought to preserve their hard-won freedom, and they succeeded.

Saint-Domingue became independent from France on January 1, 1804. The former slaves who had fought for independence changed their country's name to the Taino name Columbus had heard—Ayiti, or Haiti.

Black slaves had turned a colony controlled by white Europeans into their own independent nation. Slave owners in the United States and elsewhere were horrified. In fact, the United States did not even recognize Haiti as an independent nation until 1862. But for many slaves in the United States, the revolt was a source of inspiration and hope.

Ninety years after Haitian independence was declared, African American leader Frederick Douglass became the

In 1893, African American leader Frederick Douglass said, "We should not forget that the freedom you and I enjoy today . . . is largely due to the brave stand taken by the black sons of Haiti ninety years ago."

ambassador to Haiti. Douglass himself had once been a slave in the United States. Douglass said of the triumphant Haitian revolution: "When they struck for freedom, they built better than they knew. Their swords were not drawn and could not be drawn simply for themselves alone. . . . Striking for their freedom, they struck for the freedom of every black man in the world."

Troubled Times

In the two hundred years since becoming independent, Haitians haven't always been able to maintain their freedom. Time and again, they have fallen under the sway of violence, military rule, and dictators. Despite the turmoil, Haitians have maintained their rich culture. They continue to struggle for democracy and human rights, and to hope for a better future.

In 2006, after years of violence, Haitians went to the polls to elect a new president. Some people had to walk many miles to their polling places. At some polls, lines were already half a mile long before the voting even began. At others, voting continued after dark by candlelight. No matter how long they had to wait, many Haitians were determined to vote. They were hoping that this election would be the first step toward improving life in their beloved homeland.

The Shape of Land and Sea

Haiti's coastline is a mix of sandy beaches and steep hillsides.

H AITI COVERS THE WESTERN THIRD OF THE ISLAND OF Hispaniola. The nation of the Dominican Republic occupies the eastern two-thirds of the island. Hispaniola is also called Quisqueya, which is a Taino name that means "Cradle of Life." This was the Taino people's name for the island, and it is still used by many Haitians and their Dominican neighbors.

Hispaniola is the second largest of the islands called the Greater Antilles, which mark the northern border of the Caribbean Sea. Other islands in the chain include Cuba, Jamaica, and Puerto Rico.

The seas around Hispaniola are warm and shallow. The deepest waters lie to the west, in the 50 miles (80 kilometers) between Haiti and Cuba. Huge cargo ships head through this channel, which is called the Windward Passage.

Opposite: **A farmer tends his crops.**

The Shape of Land and Sea   **17**

Fishing boats docked in Port-au-Prince harbor. The fishing catch has declined over the years because of overfishing and pollution.

Made by Mountains

Haiti is shaped rather like a large, backward letter C. The vertical part of the C is the border with the Dominican Republic. The top and bottom parts are peninsulas that stretch out to the west. The two peninsulas are separated by the Gulf of Gonâve. Port-au-Prince Bay is at the southeastern side of the Gulf of Gonâve. Port-au-Prince, Haiti's capital and largest city, spreads out along this bay.

Hispaniola is the highest of all the Caribbean islands. About four-fifths of Haiti is covered by mountains. Its major mountain ranges include the Massif du Nord ("North Mountain Range"), the Noires ("Black") Mountains, and the Matheux Mountains. The country's southernmost range, the Massif de la Selle ("Saddle Mountain Range"), contains the country's highest point, Pic la Selle. The peak rises to 8,793 feet (2,680 meters). The Massif de la Selle extends westward into the southern peninsula as the Massif de la Hotte ("Hood Range"). Pic Macaya, the country's second-highest peak, is located there.

Some Haitian farmers cut steps into the sloping land. This makes flat fields on which to grow crops.

The nation of Haiti includes a number of small islands. Though these islands are beautiful, few people live on them because they lack adequate water. Pirates once hid out in coves on these islands.

The largest island, Gonâve Island, is about 65 miles (105 km) long. Lying in the center of Port-au-Prince Bay, it sometimes protects the capital city from storms coming from

Haiti's Geographic Features

Highest Elevation: Pic la Selle, 8,793 feet (2,680 m)

Lowest Elevation: Sea level, along the coast

Area: 10,714 square miles (27,749 sq km)

Longest River: Artibonite, 174 miles (280 km)

Largest Lake: Lake Saumâtre, 70 square miles (181 sq km)

Coastline: 1,131 miles (1,820 km)

Annual Rainfall: Ranges from 5 inches (13 cm) in the northwest to more than 145 inches (365 cm) in the southwest

Average Temperatures: 75°F (24°C) in January and 83°F (28°C) in July, with higher elevations about 10°F (5°C) cooler

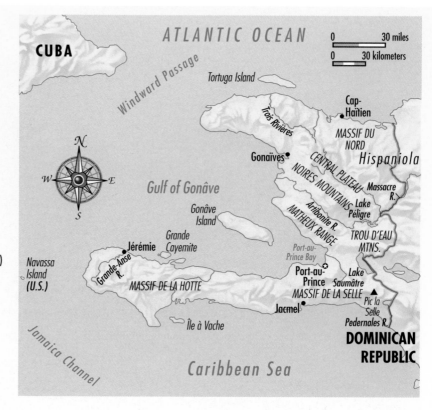

the west. Gonâve Island's barren hills are fringed by white-sand beaches and coral reefs, which draw tourists.

Tortuga Island, which lies off Haiti's northern coast, was a pirate stronghold in the seventeenth century. Mountainous and rocky, its only habitable area is on the southern coast. Île à Vache ("Cow Island") lies off Haiti's southern coast. It got its name because it was once overrun by wild cows, the descendants of animals abandoned by the Spanish. The island is becoming a popular tourist spot because of its crystal clear waters and good beaches. Two islands called Les Cayemites lie off the northern shore of the southern peninsula. The bigger one, Grande Cayemite, is inhabited.

Tortuga Island was named for the island's shape. The word *tortuga* is Spanish for "turtle."

The U.S. Island

About 35 miles (56 km) off the western end of Haiti lies Navassa Island. In 1857, the United States claimed the island because it was a source of guano, the collected droppings of seabirds, which makes excellent fertilizer. Guano was no longer harvested on the island after 1901.

The small island was declared a national wildlife refuge in 1999 to protect its diverse bird and fish populations. Today, no one lives on Navassa Island, although Haitian fishers, who insist that it belongs to Haiti, often camp there.

Lakes and Rivers

The largest lake in Haiti is Lake Saumâtre. It is located in the southeast near the Dominican border. The lake's vivid blue water is salty.

The country's longest river, the Artibonite, stretches for 174 miles (280 km) between the Noires and the Matheux mountains. A dam was built on the river in the 1950s. Water flowing over turbines in the dam produces electricity. The amount of electricity it produces is not constant, however. The river's water level drops during the dry season, limiting how much electricity the dam can produce. Most of Haiti's other rivers almost disappear during the dry season.

A wide, fertile valley spreads out from the Artibonite River. Most of Haiti's farms are located here and on the nation's other few flat plains. These are also the most densely populated regions of the country.

The Artibonite Valley is Haiti's major rice-growing region.

Many hurricanes blow across Haiti. These huge, raging storms form in the Atlantic Ocean and then often whip across the Caribbean.

In 1963, Hurricane Flora killed about 8,000 people in Haiti. This was the sixth-highest death toll from an Atlantic hurricane in recorded history. Hurricane Georges in 1998 killed fewer people, but it destroyed an estimated 80 percent of Haiti's crops. In 2004, Hurricane Jeanne flooded large parts of the country. More than 3,000 people were killed and 167,000 were left homeless.

The Vodou Waterfall

The Saut d'Eau waterfall tumbles down the steep cliffs of central Haiti. Some people believe that in the mid-1800s, an image of the Virgin Mary, the mother of Jesus, appeared there. Today, the site is important to followers of the Vodou religion. People who practice Vodou make a pilgrimage to the waterfall at least once in their lives. There, they pray to Erzulie, the goddess of love, whom many equate with Mary.

Hurricanes are particularly damaging in Haiti because so many of the nation's forests have been destroyed. With no trees to block powerful winds, hurricanes can do more damage to houses and other structures. The destruction of the forests also makes flooding worse because soil washes away easily, clogging rivers with debris.

Trees are being planted by the millions in Haiti. It will take many years, however, before they can serve as a protective buffer against hurricanes.

In 2004, Hurricane Jeanne wreaked havoc in Haiti. Ten days after the storm, many parts of the country remained flooded.

In some places, the border between the Dominican Republic and Haiti is obvious. Most trees have been cut in Haiti, while forests still stand in the Dominican Republic.

Climate

The weather in Haiti is warm year-round. The temperature changes little between winter and summer, with an average of 75 degrees Fahrenheit (24 degrees Celsius) in January and 83°F (28°C) six months later. Only the highest mountains ever get frost.

Though many storms roll across Haiti, much of the country is surprisingly dry. That's because it lies in a rain shadow. Rain shadows occur when winds meet mountains. As the wind carries clouds up the slope of the mountain, the air cools and rain falls on the side the wind is coming from. By the time that air crosses to the other side of the mountain, all the rain has fallen. On the island of Hispaniola, the Dominican Republic receives most of the rain, while Haiti lies in the dry rain shadow.

Most of the rain Haiti does get falls between March and May. This time is called the wet season. The dry season occurs from December through February. Haiti's northern peninsula is drier than its southern peninsula. Some spots in the north get less than 5 inches (13 centimeters) of rain each year.

Looking at Haiti's Cities

Port-au-Prince, Haiti's capital, is the country's largest city by far. In 2007, it was home to an estimated 1,321,522 people. Haiti's second- and third-largest cities are both suburbs of Port-au-Prince. Carrefour had a population of 482,123 people in 2007, while 422,572 people lived in Delmas.

Cap-Haïtien (right), also called Le Cap, is the nation's fourth-largest city, with a population of 142,018. Located on the northern coast, it is an important harbor for cargo and fishing. When Cap-Haïtien was founded in 1670, it was called Cap-Français. It served as the capital of the French colony of Saint-Domingue. Famous for its wealth and beauty, Le Cap was sometimes called "Little Paris." King Henri

Christophe built his palace, Sans Souci (meaning "Without Worries"), at the nearby town of Milot. Despite the city's rich history, most of its buildings date from the twentieth century. Earlier buildings were destroyed in earthquakes and fires.

Pétionville (left), the fifth-largest city, is also a suburb of Port-au-Prince. The wealthy city lies to the east of the capital.

Gonaïves, Haiti's sixth-largest city, is a seaport. Many of the country's food exports—sugar, rice, and bananas—leave through its harbor. Haitian independence was declared in Gonaïves in 1804 in a plaza now known as the Place de l'Independence. Gonaïves is a flat city, which left it vulnerable to Hurricane Jeanne in 2004. The storm flooded the city and destroyed many roads and buildings.

Threatened
Beauty

28

IT IS IMPOSSIBLE TO TALK ABOUT HAITI'S WILDLIFE WITHout first talking about its trees. When Christopher Columbus landed at what is now Haiti, he found a densely wooded land. Back then, more than 90 percent of the island of Hispaniola was forested. Today, forests cover only about 2 percent of Haiti.

Haiti's trees have long been cut down to make room for farmland and for use as building material. Haiti's original forests held mahogany and oak trees that were used by the French to make fine furniture. Haitians once used mahogany to build coffins. Today, the mahogany trees are gone, and some Haitian carpenters use the wood of the avocado tree for coffin making.

Much of the destruction of Haiti's forests happened in recent decades. Many Haitians found that wood and charcoal made from felled trees were the only cooking fuels they could

Opposite: **More than five thousand kinds of plants grow on Haiti's hilly land.**

Most of Haiti's trees have been cut down for use as fuel.

afford. The destruction sped up in the 1990s, when other countries stopped selling oil to Haiti in the hope of forcing its illegal military government from power. Without oil, Haitians had no choice but to use wood and charcoal. The desperation of the last few decades has caused most of Haiti's once-lush forests to be wiped out. Though international organizations have planted millions of trees in Haiti, so far they haven't been able to keep pace with the destruction of the forests.

Plant Life

Haiti boasts at least 5,000 species of plants. This number includes at least 160 species of orchids and several hundred kinds of ferns. Such plants are typical in warm, wet regions, but the country is also home to plant life that thrives in dry conditions. Cactuses and other hardy plants grow well in Haiti.

Cactuses thrive in Haiti's dry regions. They burst into bloom after spring rains.

Crocodiles can live as long as seventy years. They dwell in regions where freshwater and saltwater mix.

Even in the cities—perhaps mostly in the cities—the vivid blooms of frangipani, poinciana, bougainvillea, and hibiscus make everything seem alive and colorful. While many North Americans see poinsettias only in Christmas displays, Haitian poinsettia shrubs bloom most of the year.

Mangrove forests line some of Haiti's coasts. The mangrove is a remarkable kind of tree because it can live in saltwater. Long, fingerlike roots rise up out of the water, holding the mangrove trees aloft. Many creatures live among the tree roots. Fish breed there, and oysters and barnacles attach themselves to the mangrove roots. Crocodiles and birds also thrive in the mangrove forests.

At night, princess parrot fish burrow into the sand near coral reefs. They then cover themselves in a slimy substance that masks their scent, keeping them safe from predators.

Life in the Sea

Coral reefs sit in the shallow waters surrounding the Haitian mainland and its smaller islands. These underwater formations are made from the skeletons of countless tiny creatures called coral polyps. Living corals are colorful and often have soft, flexible shapes. Fish and other sea creatures make their home among the corals, and tourists flock to the reefs to see the incredible variety of life.

Green, hawksbill, and loggerhead sea turtles make frequent visits to the coral reefs. Haiti's fishers harvest conch, spiny lobster, shrimp, and parrot fish to sell at market. Divers capture colorful fish among the coral reefs for sale around the world to stock aquariums. The reefs are easily damaged, however. Pollution and changing sea temperatures can destroy a reef. Even touching a reef can damage it! If coral reefs are destroyed, the colorful reef fish will also disappear.

The West Indian manatee also faces danger. This large sea creature lives in the shallows along Haiti's west coast. Manatees are mammals, so they must come to the surface regularly to breathe. At the surface, they are easily caught in fishing nets.

Sponges are common creatures in coral reefs. Once they attach to a surface, they can never move again.

Birds

More than 260 species of birds have been seen on Hispaniola. Thirty-one of them are found only there. Birds found only on Hispaniola include the Hispaniolan trogon, the Hispaniolan parrot, and two species of palm tanagers. The La Selle thrush is severely endangered, as is the Hispaniolan crossbill.

Another bird found only on Hispaniola is the palmchat. These small, slender, brownish-green and white birds live in groups. Together, their gurgling noises make a clamor. They build huge nests in trees, often in the cities.

Garbage to Land

Haiti is expanding, especially around Port-au-Prince, but in an unfortunate way. Garbage dumped into the sea collects soil that has washed out into the water. When enough soil collects, the result is new land. As soon as the land hardens, people who live in seafront slums claim the new land and build shacks on it.

The National Bird

The Hispaniolan trogon is Haiti's national bird. About 12 inches (30 cm) long, this colorful bird has glossy green wings, a red belly, a gray throat, and a dark blue tail. The national bird was chosen by Haitian children in a popular vote. The Hispaniolan trogon is rapidly disappearing from the Massif de la Hotte.

Seabirds and shorebirds abound in Haiti. Huge, magnificent frigate birds breed in the cliffs that rise above the ocean waves. A male frigate bird has a vivid red pouch under its beak that it inflates during mating season. Another Haitian seabird, the white-tailed tropicbird, sports a narrow tail as long as its body.

The rare black-capped petrel once bred throughout the Caribbean, but now it breeds only on the cliffs of Hispaniola

Unlike most woodpeckers, Hispaniolan woodpeckers usually live in groups. This helps them protect their nests.

The Bird Man from Haiti

John James Audubon (1785–1851), a famous painter of American birds and flowers, was born at Les Cayes when Haiti was still the French colony of Saint-Domingue. He was the son of a French plantation owner and a woman of French descent who was born in Haiti. Audubon was raised in France. In his late teens, he went to live in the United States, primarily to avoid having to fight in the French army. There, he began painting birds. On his treks through America to paint birds, he discovered many new species.

The Hispaniola tree frog is the world's largest tree frog. Some are 5 inches (13 cm) long.

and perhaps on the island of Dominica. The petrels' moaning calls can be heard as they fly over the cliffs.

The roseate spoonbill and the flamingo bring splashes of bright pink to wading areas, such as Lake Saumâtre. White ibises sometimes join them in the waters.

Reptiles and Amphibians

Two large species of reptiles live in Haiti: the American crocodile and the rhinoceros iguana. The American crocodile (the same species as is found in Florida) lives around Lake Saumâtre and in some coastal rivers. The rhinoceros iguana gets its name from the three horny growths between its eyes and its nostrils. These iguanas, which can grow up to 4 feet (1.2 m) long, live in dry, rocky areas. Humans sometimes hunt the iguanas as food, which has reduced their numbers.

Haiti is home to several snake species, none of them poisonous. Snakes play an important role in Vodou. Dumballa, the father figure, is the snake god.

Many types of frogs live in Haiti, and some are severely endangered. The Morne Macay robber frog, one of the world's smallest frogs, lives only in the highest reaches of Pic Macaya. All of these tiny frogs live in one small place, and their forest habitat is rapidly declining.

Both male and female rhinoceros iguanas have three hornlike bumps above the nostrils. The iguanas are active during the day and burrow underground at night.

Mammals

Like many island nations, Haiti has no large native mammals. But two species that cause trouble for Haiti's native animals have been introduced to the island. They are the opossum and the mongoose. The mongoose is a small, catlike creature which is a danger to the black-capped petrel. It also feeds on the island's native mammals such as mice, rats, moles, and shrews.

Two of Haiti's small mammals are scarce. The Hispaniola hutia looks a little like a guinea pig. It is about 13 inches (33 cm) long, not counting its short, naked tail. As the forest

Hispaniola hutias come out mostly at night. They feed on fruit, leaves, and twigs.

habitat of these furry animals disappears, they are becoming increasingly rare. They are good to eat, so hunting has contributed to their decline.

Also endangered is the Haitian solenodon. An insect-eater related to the hedgehog and shrew, the solenodon is about the size of a large rat but has a much longer nose than a rat. The creature's bite is poisonous and sometimes fatal. The solenodon uses its snout to root around on the ground searching for food. It has strong claws for tearing open hollow logs to reach insects.

Haitian solenodons dig a maze of tunnels with their strong, sharp claws. Aboveground, they are clumsy.

The Citadelle looms over the surrounding countryside. It was built to house five thousand soldiers.

National Parks

Haiti has four national parks. One, the National History Park, incorporates several sites, including the Citadelle near Cap-Haïtien. The Citadelle is the largest fortress in the Western Hemisphere. Its walls are 13 feet (4 m) thick and reach heights of 130 feet (40 m). King Henri Christophe had the fortress built in the years leading up to 1820, to defend the country in case the French tried to retake it. The Citadelle was built with forced labor. Thousands of people had to drag huge stones up a mountain 3,000 feet (900 m) high to build the massive fortress.

Haiti's other national parks were created to preserve plants and animals. The first was Pic Macaya National Park, which was established in 1983. Pic Macaya features the country's last stand of uncut cloud forest. Cloud forests form on mountainsides that are almost always shrouded in mist. Pic Macaya abounds with plants, rare butterflies, and many species of bats.

Near the Dominican border is Pine Forest National Park (Forêt des Pines). It was created to preserve giant pine trees that are in danger of being cut down.

About 16 miles (25 km) southwest of Port-au-Prince is La Visite National Park. It contains the country's highest mountain, Pic la Selle. La Visite covers rugged country that includes cloud forests, waterfalls, and caves. The park has some areas of grassland, but nearby residents have turned many of them into cornfields. Some people also illegally cut down trees. Like so much of Haiti's natural world, La Visite's greatest threat comes from the desperate poverty of the Haitian people.

La Visite National Park holds some of Haiti's last remaining forests.

A Turbulent History

IT IS NOT CERTAIN WHICH OF THE ISLANDS IN THE BAHAMAS Christopher Columbus saw first when he chanced on the "New World" in 1492. It is known, however, that he arrived on the island of Hispaniola on December 5.

Three weeks later, on Christmas Day, one of Columbus's ships, the *Santa María*, was damaged by striking a coral reef. Columbus and his men, with some help of the curious Taino Indians, took the ship apart and built two houses. Columbus called his village La Navidad, which means "Christmas" in Spanish. A few weeks later, his men kidnapped a few Indians to show off in Spain, and Columbus sailed back to Europe.

Opposite: **Construction of the Citadelle took fifteen years.**

Christopher Columbus made his first journey to the Western Hemisphere with three ships and eighty-six men.

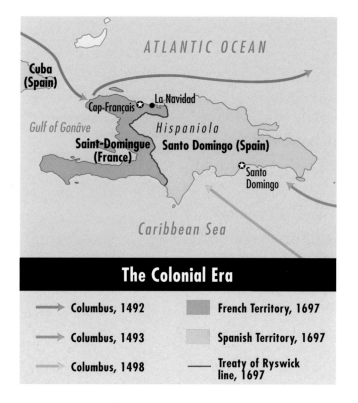

ATLANTIC OCEAN

Cuba
(Spain)

Cap-Français ✪ ● La Navidad

Gulf of Gonâve

Hispaniola

Saint-Domingue
(France)   Santo Domingo (Spain)

✪ Santo
Domingo

Caribbean Sea

The Colonial Era

→ Columbus, 1492   ▨ French Territory, 1697

→ Columbus, 1493   ▨ Spanish Territory, 1697

→ Columbus, 1498   — Treaty of Ryswick
                          line, 1697

Columbus returned the following year and found La Navidad destroyed. The men he had left there had been killed. He established a new colony, and from that moment on, Hispaniola was never without colonists. Columbus's son Diego later became governor of the colony, which was then called Santo Domingo.

The Spanish had found gold in other colonies in the Americas, so they hoped to also find some in Santo Domingo. A little gold was discovered, but the Spanish soon found a better way to make money: plantation agriculture. Plantations were large farms that generally produced only one crop. In Santo Domingo, that crop was usually sugar or indigo, a plant used to make blue dye. The Spanish forced the indigenous people to work in their fields. They also raided other parts of the Caribbean for slaves. Gradually, they began to import African slaves to work on the plantations.

France, too, established colonies on Hispaniola. The island became a pawn in the struggle between France and Spain that was going on in Europe. In 1697, the Treaty of Ryswick between the two countries gave the western third of Santo Domingo to France. The French called their part of the island Saint-Domingue, while the eastern two-thirds

Santo Domingo was the first Spanish colony in the Americas. The Spaniards killed any indigenous people who refused to accept their rule.

remained Santo Domingo. From that time, the two parts of the island began to develop major differences, which would lead to much conflict.

The Buccaneers

In the 1600s, the islands around Saint-Domingue, especially Tortuga, were attractive hiding places for pirates who roamed the Caribbean in search of Spanish gold. The most famous was Henry Morgan, who came from Great Britain. He gathered two thousand pirates on Tortuga. From there, he headed for Panama to steal the riches the Spanish had stored there.

Some pirates on Tortuga sailed the short 10 miles (16 km) across the passage to what is now Haiti to hunt wild cattle and pigs. They used a method called *boucan* to smoke the meat of the animals they killed. Thus, they came to be called *boucaniers*. That French word was turned into the English *buccaneers*. Caribbean pirates have been known by this name ever since.

Haitians in the American Revolution

During the American Revolution, the British captured the city of Savannah, Georgia. On October 9, 1779, Americans and their French allies fought a battle to try to free the city from British control. A band of perhaps eight hundred free black Haitians fought alongside them. It is said that among them was a fourteen-year-old drummer boy who later became Henry Christophe, the leader of free Haiti. The attack failed, and Savannah was not freed from British control until 1782. Still, the soldiers from Haiti fought bravely, and a monument honoring their efforts is planned for Savannah.

The Haitian Revolution

Saint-Domingue quickly become the most profitable colony in the Americas, primarily because of slave labor. Called "the Pearl of the Antilles," it was the world's leading producer of sugar and coffee in the late eighteenth century. It also produced indigo, rum, and some cotton. Saint-Domingue produced more wealth for France than all the North American colonies together did for Britain. By 1780, there were five hundred thousand black slaves in Saint-Domingue. They were controlled by a white population of only thirty thousand.

France acquired great wealth from the slave labor that sustained sugar plantations in Saint-Domingue.

In Saint-Domingue, slaves had long resisted and rebelled by running away from the plantations or poisoning their masters. In 1789, word of the French Revolution came from Europe. The revolution brought upheaval to the colony. Free black men and people of mixed race (sometimes called mulattoes) wondered about the possibility of equality. At the same time, the white planters of French descent, called Creoles, hoped to gain more control over their local affairs from France. The idea of rebellion against the established way of life was in the air.

A massive slave uprising—the largest ever in the Americas—began on the night of August 21, 1791. It would eventually lead to Haitian independence.

On August 14, 1791, a Vodou priest named Dutty Boukman held a ceremony in which he asked the gods to help the slaves in an uprising that many were planning. He urged those present to "listen to the voice of liberty" that spoke within them.

A week later, slaves began to rise up. In the first two months, the slaves killed more than two thousand white people and burned at least a thousand plantations. Many white planters fled the island. Officials and troops were sent from France to try to suppress the revolt, but they failed. Boukman was killed in battle, but other leaders took his place, and the rebellion was never defeated.

The Spanish, who hoped to win Saint-Domingue from the French, gave support to the slave rebels in the colony. Toussaint Louverture, one the leaders of the rebellion, became an officer in the Spanish army and fought against the French during this period. In 1793, the rebels claimed victory when the new French government abolished slavery in the colony. Louverture then joined the French army.

In 1800, Louverture turned his troops against the Spanish, taking possession of neighboring Santo Domingo for France. The following year, he proclaimed himself governor-for-life

The Founder of Haiti

François Dominique Toussaint Louverture was born on a plantation around 1743. He learned to read, and in time he was put in charge of all livestock on the plantation. In 1777, he was given his freedom and may even have owned slaves and land. After joining the slave rebellion, he quickly became known for being able to find ways through the enemy lines that didn't appear to exist. This talent won him the name Louverture, which means "The Opening." He added it to the end of his name.

Louverture helped lead the rebels to victory in 1793, when slavery was abolished in the colony. Afterward, he became the colony's most important leader. In 1802, French leader Napoléon Bonaparte sent in troops to try to take away his power. After fighting the French for several months, Louverture surrendered with the guarantee that he would be able to retire peacefully. But French troops tricked and captured him. They sent him to France, where he died in prison on April 7, 1803, nine months before Haiti declared its independence.

Many people around the world were impressed by Louverture and appalled by his capture and death in prison. English poet William Wordsworth even wrote a poem about the event.

Haitian schoolchildren learn by heart the words Louverture uttered when he was forced onto the ship that would carry him to prison in France: "In overthrowing me, you have cut down in Saint-Domingue only the tree of liberty. It will spring up again by the roots for they are numerous and deep."

and declared that slavery was forever abolished in Saint-Domingue. Louverture worked to rebuild parts of the plantation economy of Saint-Domingue. Many white planters who had fled returned to the colony.

By the early 1800s, however, Napoléon Bonaparte, the general who had taken control of France, was considering returning slavery to the colonies. He sent a fleet of ships and thousands of soldiers to Saint-Domingue. Louverture's troops were at first defeated. He was captured and sent to France, where he died in prison.

Realizing that Bonaparte intended to reenslave them, the people of Saint-Domingue fought courageously against the French army in many months of brutal battles.

After Louverture was taken to France, his right-hand man, Jean-Jacques Dessalines, became the leader of the revolution. He and his troops defeated the French at the Battle of Vertières in 1803. It would be the final battle in the only successful slave rebellion in world history.

A New Nation

On January 1, 1804, at the city of Gonaïves, Dessalines declared Haiti an independent nation. Haiti was

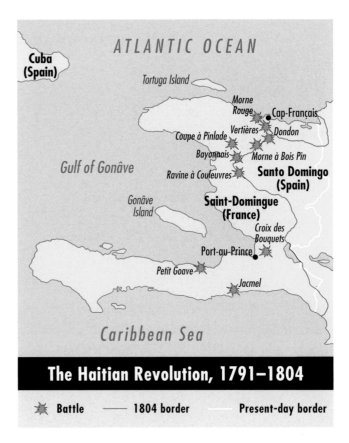

The Haitian Revolution, 1791–1804

✳ Battle   —— 1804 border   —— Present-day border

only the second country in the Western Hemisphere to gain its independence. The first was the United States.

In the new Haiti, white men were forbidden to own property. Most whites had fled during the last years of the Haitian Revolution, but some remained. Dessalines claimed that they were hoping to regain control of the country, and he ordered many of them massacred. He allowed a small number of white people to become Haitian citizens. Because he had declared that all Haitians were black, he had turned these whites, officially, into black people.

Haiti's first constitution, in 1805, made Dessalines emperor. He tried to break up large land-holdings in the country and distribute them to former slaves. These efforts made him some enemies, and he was murdered in 1806.

After Dessalines's death, two other leaders from the revolution fought for control. After a brief civil war, Henri Christophe and Alexandre Pétion divided Haiti between them. Christophe ruled as a king in the north. Pétion created a democratic republic in the south, which he called the Republic of Haiti.

Pétion was president of the Republic of Haiti until 1818. He chose Jean-Pierre Boyer, a mulatto who had fought with Louverture, as

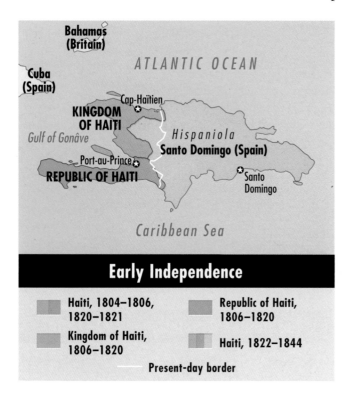

Early Independence

Haiti, 1804–1806, 1820–1821	Republic of Haiti, 1806–1820
Kingdom of Haiti, 1806–1820	Haiti, 1822–1844
— Present-day border	

The King of Haiti

Henri Christophe was born on the island of Grenada in 1757. He went to Saint-Domingue as a teenager and later became one of Toussaint Louverture's lieutenants in the war for independence. In 1811, he declared himself king of Haiti. Seeking respect from foreign powers, he built a large palace at Sans Souci and a fort called the Citadelle. He forcibly recruited many laborers to build his projects, and some died doing the hard work. After suffering a stroke that left him unable to lead, Christophe committed suicide in 1820—with a silver bullet, it is said.

The Republic's President

Alexandre Pétion was born in Port-au-Prince in 1770, the son of a black mother and a French father, who was white. After training as a soldier in France, he worked with Jean-Jacques Dessalines to unify blacks and mulattoes to fight for independence against the French. He was elected president in 1806 and again in 1811 and 1815. He decided that it was too hard to work with a democratically elected government and had himself declared president-for-life in 1816. He died two years later of yellow fever.

his successor. Christophe died in 1820, and Boyer succeeded in combining northern and southern Haiti later that year.

Jean-Pierre Boyer became president in 1818. The nation's economy floundered during his years in office, and he was forced to leave the country in 1843.

A Century of Change

In 1822, Haiti gathered its troops and occupied neighboring Santo Domingo. For twenty-two years, the entire island was one nation, though partly French and partly Spanish. Dominicans often think of those years as ones of slavery and oppression, but, in fact, Haiti abolished slavery in Spanish Hispaniola. As taxes rose, however, a revolution began in Spanish Haiti. In 1844, the region succeeded in breaking away and became an independent nation, the Dominican Republic.

Between 1843 and 1915, Haiti had twenty-two different heads of state. New leaders often took charge violently.

Meanwhile, Haitians rebuilt the coffee economy, which had declined during the revolution. Attracted by the nation's agricultural possibilities, U.S. companies began buying up land and investing money in the country. The U.S. government was also becoming more involved in Haitian affairs.

U.S. troops set sail for Haiti in 1915. American troops remained in Haiti until 1934, making this the longest U.S. occupation of a foreign nation.

The U.S. Occupation

In the early twentieth century, U.S. Navy ships sailed into Haitian waters many times. The United States insisted that the ships were there to protect American lives and property. Then, in 1915, U.S. president Woodrow Wilson gave the go-ahead for an invasion of Haiti. The United States and Germany were about to become enemies in World War I, and Wilson claimed that Germany might gain control of Haiti. The occupation was brutal. American Marines killed thousands of Haitians who objected to their presence.

The United States stayed in Haiti for almost twenty years. It imposed a new constitution on the people, one that allowed Americans to own anything they wanted. During the occupation, Americans back home protested the violent acts some marines had committed against Haitians who resisted them. The U.S. forces in Haiti created a national guard that became the Haitian army. The Haitian soldiers were often as guilty of brutality as the U.S. Marines had been.

Massacre

From 1930 to 1961, the Dominican Republic was under the control of dictator Rafael Trujillo. In the 1930s, he decided to reinforce the border with Haiti, and to force the many Haitian farmers and workers who lived in the Dominican Republic to go home.

In October 1937, Trujillo ordered his soldiers to identify the immigrants and murder them. About twelve thousand Haitians were killed. Haitian novelist Edwidge Danticat wrote a book about the event called *The Farming of Bones*.

The occupation did have some positive effects. The deadly disease called yellow fever was wiped out. Hospitals, schools, and roads were built, though often using forced labor. Unfortunately, all the roads led to Port-au-Prince, which isolated the countryside. This is still a problem today.

The U.S. occupation finally ended in 1934. Haiti was once again in control of its own affairs.

Haiti's Golden Age

In 1946, Dumarsais Estimé became president. Under his leadership, the minimum wage was raised and some of the nation's loans were paid off.

At the time, Haiti was an important banana producer. The bananas were grown by the American-owned Standard Fruit Company. Estimé nationalized the banana business in Haiti, meaning that the government took over ownership of it. This angered some powerful people, and his government was ousted by a military group led by Colonel Paul Magloire. Magloire was then elected president and ruled from 1950 to 1956, in what has been called Haiti's "golden age of peace." He briefly turned Haiti into a popular tourist destination.

The Duvalier Years

By 1957, Haiti was bankrupt. After Magloire left office, the country endured six different governments in ten months. In the first peaceful election, held in September 1957, François Duvalier was chosen president. Duvalier was a doctor, and he was known as "Papa Doc." From Duvalier's six-year term as president would spring decades of dictatorship.

Duvalier's years were filled with terror and violence. Papa Doc's sunglass-wearing thugs, called the Tontons Macoutes, killed an estimated twenty thousand to fifty thousand Haitians. Their name came from a Haitian children's nursery rhyme about a bogeyman who steals naughty children. Between 1957 and 1971, about four-fifths of Haiti's professionals—

François Duvalier came to power in 1957. Seven years later he declared himself president-for-life.

doctors, teachers, and the like—fled the country. Haiti has never recovered from the loss.

Several attempts were made to remove Duvalier from power. These attempts usually involved fighters from other islands and Haitian exiles from the United States and the Dominican Republic. The Tontons Macoutes mercilessly killed those who tried to oust Duvalier.

Duvalier died in 1971 and was replaced by his son, Jean-Claude "Baby Doc" Duvalier. Baby Doc was no better than his father. He was forced out of power in 1986, and the military took over again.

Duvalier Father and Son

François Duvalier (below), nicknamed "Papa Doc," was born in Port-au-Prince in 1907. He trained as a physician and wrote about Haitian culture. His clothing and style recalled Baron Samedi, the Vodou god of the dead. With the backing of the army, he was elected president in 1957 and then declared himself president-for-life. He received support from the United States throughout his regime.

His son, Jean-Claude (above), was called "Baby Doc." He came to power in 1971 at age nineteen. Like his father, Baby Doc declared himself president-for-life, though much of the political decision making was done by his mother. In 1986, a widespread uprising began against the younger Duvalier. The United States realized that he had lost control of the country and pressured him to leave. Duvalier went to France, taking with him huge amounts of money belonging to the Haitian government. He still lives in France and even now suggests that it would be good for Haiti if he returned.

Aristide, Priest and President

Jean-Bertrand Aristide was born in 1953 in a small town on Haiti's southern coast. His father died when he was an infant, and his family soon moved to Port-au-Prince. Growing up, he was educated by Roman Catholic priests, and he himself became a priest in 1982. His political activities quickly became a problem for the church. He always sided with the poor and encouraged them to rise up against the Duvalier dictatorship. In 1988, he was forced to leave the priesthood.

Aristide ran for president in 1990. His backers convinced many peasants to vote for the first time, and Aristide won by a huge margin. He did not have the support of the legislature, however, and the military soon forced him out. In 2001, Aristide again became president. Again, he was forced out of power. He now

lives in South Africa and, for the moment, at least, is unable to return to Haiti.

A Violent Democracy

Four years of military rule ended when Jean-Bertrand Aristide was elected president in December 1990. It was Haiti's first democratic election in decades. The following September, another military coup, this one backed by business leaders, forced Aristide to leave the country. Three years later, Haiti's military leaders agreed to allow Aristide to return if he agreed that they would not be charged with his overthrow. By September 1994, Aristide was once again in power.

He had only a year left as president. His prime minister, René Préval, won the next election for president. Aristide ran for president again in 2000. The poor supported him, and he won the election, taking office in 2001.

Suspected thieves are rounded up by rebels in Cap-Haïtien. Rebel forces took over northern Haiti in January 2004.

Aristide's popular support gradually disappeared, however, as his government did not reduce poverty or stop the killings and drug trafficking that made life so difficult for the Haitian people. Opposition to him grew both inside and outside Haiti, and violence spread. By January 2004, rebels had captured the north. As they made their way toward Port-au-Prince, they killed their opponents and burned down police stations. Aristide fled the capital on February 29, 2004. Some say he left voluntarily; others say he was handcuffed and forced onto an airplane.

Violence continued during the following months. The United Nations, an organization made up of countries from around the world dedicated to settling conflicts peacefully, sent in peacekeeping troops to help calm the turmoil. They were not able to stop the bloodshed, but they did oversee a new election in 2006.

During the campaign, people loyal to Aristide blocked roads with burning tires and rioted around the capital city. Préval was declared the winner of the election.

A New Chance

In the summer of 2006, France and Canada began working together to help rebuild Haiti. Other countries joined in. Haiti is plagued by many ills: environmental problems, poor educational and health systems, few jobs, and terrible violence. Much effort by people the world over will be necessary to help Haiti claim its place as a peaceful modern country.

UN peacekeepers keep an eye on a demonstration in Port-au-Prince. In 2007, more than eight thousand UN troops and police were stationed in Haiti.

The Changeable Government

HAITI WAS THE FIRST BLACK REPUBLIC IN THE WORLD and only the second republic in the Western Hemisphere. Despite being two hundred years old, Haiti's democratic system has often broken down. During the nineteenth century, at least ten leaders declared themselves president-for-life. The military has taken over the government several times. Only rarely in the country's long history has one elected leader followed another elected leader.

Haiti has had twenty-two constitutions in the two hundred years since independence, but they have seldom been followed. The current constitution was approved in March 1987, but it was suspended the following June. It has often been suspended and then put back into effect in the years since then.

The military police headquarters is in Port-au-Prince.

The Haitian Flag

In 1803, during the war against the French, Jean-Jacque Dessalines's men fought under the French flag, which they had also fought under in earlier years as part of the French army. A newspaper article claimed that this meant that they were not fighting for independence. Instead, the article said, they were willing to stay part of France. Dessalines and others wanted to make sure people knew this wasn't true. They took the French flag, which has stripes of blue, white, and red, and tore the white stripe from the middle. This left a flag made of two broad stripes of red and blue.

In the center of Haiti's current flag is the Haitian coat of arms. This shows a palm tree surrounded by flags and cannons. Below this image is the motto *L'Union fait la force* ("In union there is strength").

All Haitians at least eighteen years old can vote. Women were not given the right to vote until 1950, when it was demanded by the United Nations.

A woman fills out a ballot during the 2006 presidential election.

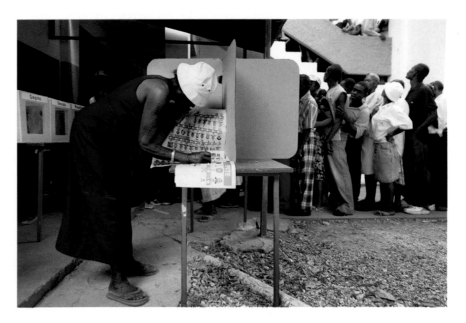

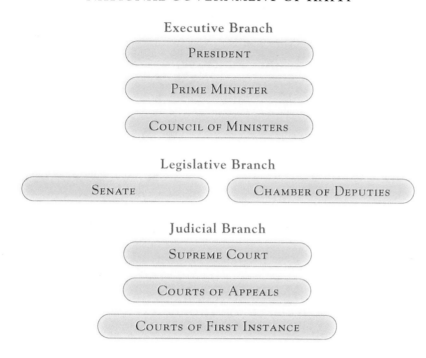

NATIONAL GOVERNMENT OF HAITI

Executive Branch

- PRESIDENT
- PRIME MINISTER
- COUNCIL OF MINISTERS

Legislative Branch

- SENATE
- CHAMBER OF DEPUTIES

Judicial Branch

- SUPREME COURT
- COURTS OF APPEALS
- COURTS OF FIRST INSTANCE

The Executive Branch

Haiti's head of state is the president, who is elected for a five-year term and may not serve two terms in a row. The president must be a landowner in Haiti.

The head of government is the prime minister, who is chosen by the president from the major political party of the National Assembly, Haiti's legislature. The choice must be approved by the National Assembly. The various divisions in the government are run by ministers, who are chosen by the prime minister. They make up the Council of Ministers, which must include at least ten people.

The First Woman at the Top

In 1990, Ertha Pascal-Trouillot, the chief justice of the Supreme Court, was appointed provisional president of Haiti after a military takeover. She was Haiti's first female president. Pascal-Trouillot held the position for almost a year, until Jean-Bertrand Aristide won democratic elections. She is the author of Haiti's most used legal reference book.

The offices of the Council of Ministers are in the ministry building in Port-au-Prince.

The Legislative Branch

Haiti's legislature, or lawmaking body, is called the National Assembly. It is made up of two houses, the Chamber of Deputies and the Senate.

The Senate has a total of thirty members. Haiti is divided into ten departments, which are something like states or provinces. Each department elects three senators. The senators serve six-year terms and can be reelected. Generally, one-third of the senators are up for election every two years.

The Senate proposes judges to be on the Supreme Court, but the Senate itself can also serve as a High Court of Justice. That might occur if, for example, the president or a minister were charged with crimes.

Haiti's departments are divided into smaller units called communes, which are usually made up of a town and the surrounding suburbs and countryside. Each commune elects at least one deputy to the Chamber of Deputies. The chamber usually has ninety-nine members. They are elected to four-year terms.

The Courts and Police

Haiti's top court is the Supreme Court. Below it are the courts of appeals. Judges on both the Supreme Court and the courts of appeals are appointed for ten years. Courts of first instance are where major cases are tried. Their justices are appointed for seven years. At the local level are justice of the peace courts, which handle minor matters.

The Price of Speaking Out

Jean Dominique (1930–2000) was a Haitian mulatto who left the privileged world he grew up in to work with poverty-stricken peasants. He trained in Paris, France, as an agronomist, an expert in agriculture.

He wanted to help Haiti's peasants find new ways to earn a living.

Dominique became a journalist and a radio commentator, speaking out against injustice. He broadcast in Creole, the language spoken by the average Haitian, rather than in French, the language of the elite. No one had ever done that before. Dominique wrote against the dictatorships that tore his country apart, and was sometimes jailed for his activities. He twice fled the country, but he always returned to help his people.

In 2000, Dominique was murdered. His killers have never been caught. Thousands of people attended his funeral, which was held in a sports stadium. *The Agronomist*, a documentary film about Dominique's life, was released in 2003.

Being a judge in Haiti is an uncertain and sometimes dangerous job. The government has frequently removed judges from their positions. Some judges have even been murdered. Given all of Haiti's political turmoil, many judges are not fair and independent. Instead, some have fallen under the control of one political faction or another. Many Haitians do not trust the judicial system any more than they trust the police.

Haiti's constitution calls for separation of the police and the military. But the two groups have often been combined, especially when dictators were in power. In these times, the military has been used to enforce the laws. Throughout much of the country's history, the military has also controlled the judicial system. During the military takeover of 1991, the

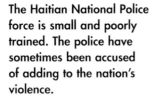
The Haitian National Police force is small and poorly trained. The police have sometimes been accused of adding to the nation's violence.

Haiti's National Anthem

The national anthem is "La Dessalinienne," or "Song of Dessalines." The words were written by Justin Lhérisson and the music by Nicolas Geffrard.

The writer and composer won a 1903 competition to write an anthem to celebrate Haiti's hundredth birthday.

French lyrics

Pour le Pays,
Pour les Ancêtres,
Marchons unis, Marchons unis.
Dans nos rangs point de traîtres!
Du sol soyons seuls maîtres.
Marchons unis, Marchons unis
Pour le Pays, Pour les Ancêtres,
Marchons, marchons, marchons unis,
Pour le Pays, Pour les Ancêtres.

English lyrics

For our Country,
For our Ancestors,
Let's march in unity, let's march in unity.
In our ranks no traitors!
We shall be the sole masters of our land.
Let's march in unity, Let's march in unity,
For our Country, for our Ancestors,
Let's march, Let's march, Let's march in unity,
For our Country, for our Ancestors.

court system collapsed and no trials were held. Thousands of people were thrown into prison with no hope of getting out.

After Jean-Bertrand Aristide returned to power in 1994, the armed forces were disbanded. A new police force called the Haitian National Police became the only security force. There are not nearly enough police to do the job. There are about five thousand policemen for eight million people. By contrast, New York City, with approximately the same population, has nearly thirty-eight thousand police!

In reality, the government of Haiti has been unable to provide many of the services that governments generally offer. It does not provide security, education, safe drinking water, electricity, health care, or hope. These needs are unlikely to be met until people's safety can be guaranteed.

Port-au-Prince: Did You Know This?

The capital of Haiti is located on Port-au-Prince Bay. A small city just a few decades ago, Port-au-Prince has now expanded up the surrounding mountainsides. Several of its suburbs, including Pétionville and Carrefour, are among the largest cities in the country. About one-fourth of the people in Haiti live in Port-au-Prince and its suburbs.

Port-au-Prince was founded in 1749 when the ship *Prince* arrived in the bay. The main street through the city is Boulevard Jean-Jacques Dessalines. The Iron Market (above), located on Dessalines, is a huge building containing hundreds of little shops and booths that sell everything from fish to sculptures. The market called Croix-des-Bossales is named for the slaves newly arrived from Africa (*bossales*) who were sold there long ago. Today, it sells fruits and vegetables.

Port-au-Prince's main streets are lined with majestic palm trees. Downtown is frantically busy during the day, with street vendors everywhere. Because Port-au-Prince has no major lighted roads, at night the city turns into a quiet ghost town.

Port-au-Prince's most important sites include the National Palace, where the president lives. It is a long white building with three rounded domes. On the huge plaza in front of the palace is the Monument to the Unknown Maroon. The word *maroon* once meant a fugitive slave. Colonies of maroons hid out in the mountains surrounding Port-au-Prince. The monument in front of the palace reminds everyone of the slaves who fought to end slavery. The dramatic statue was sculpted by Haitian artist Albert Mangonès.

To the east of the National Palace are the Panthéon Museum and the Museum of Haitian Art. The Panthéon exhibits the anchor of Christopher Columbus's flagship, the *Santa María*.

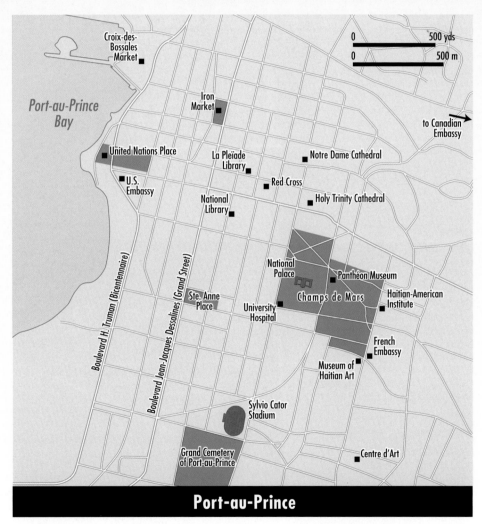

Port-au-Prince

Manufacturing
Hope

WHENEVER HAITI MAKES THE NEWS, JOURNALISTS almost always tack on the phrase "the poorest country in the Western Hemisphere." This is unfortunately true, but Haitians and other people around the world are determined to change that. It will be a long struggle.

Haiti's economic problems started long ago. Saint-Domingue was France's richest colony. It produced indigo, coffee, and sugar. After Haiti became independent, France

Opposite: **Fishing boats and nets line a beach.**

About 80 percent of Haitians live in poverty.

repeatedly tried to find a way to regain control of its former colony. Haitian president Jean-Pierre Boyer wanted France to recognize Haitian independence. Finally, in 1825, France agreed, but only on the condition that Haiti pay France for its losses. Haiti accepted France's demands, which meant that just when the young country should have been building a strong, new economy, it remained in debt to France.

Today, the average income per person in Haiti is about four hundred dollars a year. That's little more than one dollar a day. The average Haitian must survive for a full year on what the average American spends in ten days. More than two-thirds of adult Haitians are unemployed or do not have regular jobs.

The poverty rate in Haiti is higher today than it was in 1980.

What wealth the Haitian people have is not spread around evenly. About 5 percent of Haitians are French-speaking whites (Creoles) or people of mixed black and white ancestry (mulattoes). That 5 percent owns half the country's wealth.

Agriculture

When slavery ended in Haiti, the big, single-crop plantations were broken up into many small farms. Today, the average farm is only 4.4 acres (1.8 hectares). Most of the land is too steep to be good farmland. There is little rich soil, and what soil there is washes away when it rains. All of this makes it difficult for the 66 percent of Haitians who work in agriculture to make a living.

Coffee plantations yield about one-fifth of Haiti's agricultural exports. Mangoes and cacao are also grown for export. The area around the Artibonite River is an important rice-growing region.

About thirty thousand Haitians harvest the waters around Haiti instead of farming the land. Fishers take in about 6,000 tons (5,500 metric tons) of fish each year, plus another 1.7 tons (1.5 metric tons) of sea creatures such as lobster and conch. These catches provide about 50 percent of the protein that Haitians eat.

CUBA

ATLANTIC OCEAN

Tortuga Island

Cap-Haïtien

Coffee

Mangoes

Au

Cacao

Fish

Cu

Gonaïves

Mangoes

Gulf of Gonâve

Rice

Lig

Coffee

Gonâve Island

Lobster

Bananas

Rice

Jérémie

Cem

Marb

Fish

Port-au-Prince

Sugarcane Mangoes

Bx

Marb

Marb

Fish

Coffee

Jacmel

Lobster

Caribbean Sea

DOMINICAN REPUBLIC

Resources

Cropland	Forests
Diversified tropical crops	Livestock

Au	Gold	Cem	Cement	Lig	Lignite
Bx	Bauxite	Cu	Copper	Marb	Marble

Sugarcane production in Haiti has fallen in recent years. Production in 2002 was one-third of production in 1982.

Industry and Mining

Only about 9 percent of Haitians work in industry. By way of contrast, 24 percent of workers in the neighboring Dominican Republic have industrial jobs.

What Haiti Grows, Makes, and Mines

Agriculture (2000)

Sugarcane	800,000 metric tons
Cassava	338,000 metric tons
Bananas	323,000 metric tons

Manufacturing

Textiles	$183,000,000

Mining

Sand and gravel (2004)	1,000,000 metric tons

In general, the factories in Haiti are owned by foreigners. Most items manufactured are made for export. Electronics items are put together in Haiti, as is clothing. Some Haitian women are expert at detailed beadwork.

Mining plays only a small role in the Haitian economy. The country has few natural resources beyond gravel, limestone, and sand for building. In the past, some bauxite and copper were mined. Haiti has a little gold, but it has not been mined.

Baseballs

In the 1980s and 1990s, 90 percent of the world's baseballs were made in Haiti, even though baseball isn't a popular sport in the country. The balls were made for U.S. companies that took advantage of Haiti's cheap labor and tax benefits. The balls were hand-sewn by women who earned more than the average Haitian farmer. Because of Haiti's recent political instability, most baseball production—and other manufacturing jobs—have left Haiti. Much of the baseball manufacturing industry moved to Costa Rica. Some Haitians went there to teach the new workers the skill of making baseballs.

Small Loans Make a Big Difference

In 2000, Sogebank, Haiti's largest commercial bank, began to provide small loans to women who wanted to start their own businesses. Even tiny loans could make a huge difference for women who simply needed to buy supplies to get a food stand or other shop up and running. The idea for such "microloans" came from the impoverished Asian nation of Bangladesh, where it has been a great success. Muhammad Yunus, the economist who came up with the idea, won the 2006 Nobel Peace Prize for his work.

In Haiti, Sogebank had about eight thousand clients by 2006. The average loan balance was equal to about US$900. The vast majority of the loans are repaid in full and on time. Other Haitian banks are also offering microloans, giving hope to women who are trying to provide for their families.

The Need for Energy

In the 1950s, Haiti built a huge dam to produce electricity for the Artibonite Valley. But much of the country does not have a regular supply of electricity. Most homes, at least beyond Port-au-Prince, are lighted by kerosene. Oil is hard to come by in Haiti.

Lake Peligre formed when a hydroelectric dam was built in central Haiti. Thousands of people had to move because the lake flooded their land.

Why is oil so important? Because Haitians have destroyed their forests by cutting down trees to make charcoal, which they use as fuel. Charcoal is made by burning wood without using any air. The charcoal weighs less and burns hotter than wood itself. Scientists are working to find alternatives to wood-based charcoal for people in poor countries. They hope to develop ways to make charcoal out of compressed recycled paper or, perhaps, sugarcane waste.

People standing atop a tap-tap as they wait for it to depart. The buses usually leave only when they are full.

Transportation

Visitors to Port-au-Prince often notice that the sky over the city is clear and beautiful. That is because Haiti has few cars and trucks, so it has little air pollution. Though there are fewer cars than in most countries, the roads can be chaotic. Drivers tend to make up their own rules.

Instead of traditional city buses, Haiti has open-topped vans and trucks called tap-taps. They are often crowded to overflowing. Tap-taps are usually painted in eye-catching colors and designs.

Port-au-Prince has the largest port in Haiti.

Beyond the capital, less than 20 percent of the country's roads are paved. About half of these roads become unusable during the rainy season.

Port-au-Prince is a major port, with harbor facilities that can handle huge ships. The Royal Caribbean Cruise Line makes brief stops in Haiti. The ships come in to Labadie Nord, a peninsula near Cap-Haïtien. Vacationers there enjoy the sea and beaches.

Haiti has twelve airports. The largest is Port-au-Prince International Airport, located north of the city. Only three other airports have paved runways. Haiti once had a national railway line, but its tracks have disappeared into the brush. There are no passenger trains in Haiti today. The only rail service is used to transport farm products.

Haitian Currency

Haiti's basic unit of currency is the gourde. It is divided into 100 centimes. The gourde was named for real gourds—dried hard shells of a squashlike fruit. King Henri Christophe paid peasant farmers with gourds.

Paper bills have values of 1, 2, 5, 10, 25, 50, 100, and 250 gourdes. The main coins used are 50 centimes, 1 gourde, and 5 gourdes. Through much of Haiti's recent history, the value of the gourde was linked to the U.S. dollar (usually at 5 gourdes to 1 dollar).

Thus the 5-gourde coin is sometimes called 1 Haitian dollar. In 1989, this link was cut, and by 2007, US$1 was worth 39 gourdes, and 1 gourde was equal to about 2½ U.S. cents.

Haitian money depicts important people and places in Haitian history. For example, the 10-gourde note shows Catherine Flon, the woman who in 1803 sewed the first Haitian flag. The 100-gourde note shows King Henri Christophe and the Citadelle.

There are only about thirty telephones per thousand people in the country. It is estimated that only about 1 percent of Haitians have Internet access.

Every town of any size has several radio stations. Most information in Haiti is spread via radio because only about half the people can read. Radios and newspapers must toe the line with whatever political group is in power. The government-owned Haitian television network, Télévision Nationale d'Haiti (TNH), broadcasts in French, English, and Creole. Privately owned cable service was started in 1997.

Haiti has several newspapers. *Le Matin* is a daily news-paper published in French, as is *Le Nouvelliste*. *Haiti Progres* is the largest weekly paper, published in French, English, and Creole.

Some villages in Haiti have only one television. Everyone in the village shares it.

Volunteers clean up a street in Port-au-Prince. People hope that peace, and a cleaner environment, will draw tourists to Haiti.

Haiti's Economic Future

Many experts believe that the best way for Haiti to improve economically is to encourage tourism. This is an uphill battle. The country is politically unstable. It is overpopulated, and its environment is deteriorating. But the island's natural beauty offers hope.

Today, environmentalists from all over the world are trying to help protect parts of Haiti. They are also trying to educate the country's farmers about the need to preserve trees and wild lands. Only when the plants, animals, and lands are preserved, and the violence stops, are tourists going to find Haiti a desirable place to visit.

The People of Haiti

WHEN CHRISTOPHER COLUMBUS REACHED HISPANIOLA in 1492, he thought he was in India, so he called the people who greeted him Indians. The term *Indian* has been used ever since for the indigenous peoples of the Americas. He called the specific people he met on the island *Taino*, meaning "Friendly People." This may have been a reaction to the less friendly Carib people he had met earlier on other islands.

Within fifty years of Columbus's arrival, Spaniards had nearly wiped out the Taino people of Hispaniola. They began bringing in African slaves. This action would change the history of the island, and of Haiti.

Opposite: **More than 40 percent of Haitians are under fifteen years old.**

The vast majority of Haitians are of African descent.

Ethnic Haiti

Black	95%
White or mulatto	5%

In 2006, an estimated 8,308,504 people were living in Haiti. About 95 percent of Haiti's people are dark-skinned. They are the descendants of African slaves imported by the Spanish and the French. The remaining 5 percent are people of European ancestry or of mixed European and African ancestry. The latter are sometimes called mulattoes.

Skin color is important to Haitians. The lighter a man's skin and the straighter his hair, the more likely it is that others will assume he is intelligent and wealthy. Over the centuries, lighter-skinned people have held much of the power in Haiti. They have often been in conflict with the darker-skinned majority.

Haitians tend to have dark skin. Most people with lighter skin, like this woman, are part of the country's elite.

Most signs in Haiti are written in Haitian Creole. This sign urges parents to have their children vaccinated.

Language

Most Haitians speak a language called Creole, which is spelled Kréyòl in Haiti. Creole evolved from French and African languages into its own language over the course of many years. Throughout most of Haitian history, however, the nation's official language was French. Perhaps only 5 percent of Creole speakers also spoke French. And French speakers did not necessarily understand Creole.

Creole speakers were certain that French speakers looked down on them for using a language of the streets. French, meanwhile, was the language of business and government. The few who could speak both French and Creole were elite. Thus, Haitians fell into two separate groups, the elite few and everyone else, who made up a huge lower class.

Two Sides of an Island

Hispaniola is an unusual island in that it is divided between two countries. Inevitably, Haiti and the Dominican Republic are often compared. Here's how they stacked up in 2005:

	Haiti	Dominican Republic
Total population	8.3 million	8.8 million
Population density	119 per square mile (307/sq km)	71 per square mile (83/sq km)
Life expectancy at birth	52 years	68 years
Adult literacy rate	51%	88%
Primary school enrollment	54%	92%
Forested land	2%	28%
Per person income per year	$400	$7,500

This began to change during the U.S. occupation of Haiti in the early twentieth century. Haitians of all backgrounds were shocked by the racism of the occupiers. Many Haitians, even the most educated, began to take more pride in their culture and in the Creole language. The first Creole newspaper appeared in 1943. In the 1950s, a poet and playwright named Felix Morisseau-Leroy wrote a Creole version of the ancient Greek drama *Antigone*. Few Haitians had ever seen a play in their own language before.

Soon after *Antigone* was staged, a movement started to make Creole an official language in Haiti along with French. Creole was finally allowed in schools in 1978. Ten years later, in the constitution of 1987, Creole was made an official language.

Creole Words and Phrases

Wi	Yes
Non	No
Mesi	Thank you
Souple	Please
Prese prese!	Hurry!
Jodia	Today
Konben?	How much?

People at Risk

So many doctors and nurses left Haiti during recent political instability that lack of health care became a serious problem. It became even more serious when AIDS, the often fatal disease caused by a virus called HIV, spread around the world starting in the late 1970s. By the mid-1990s, people in other countries were beginning to get treatment for the disease, but the poverty in Haiti made it difficult for AIDS patients to get medicines.

An estimated three hundred thousand people in Haiti are infected with HIV. Many do not get the medical care they need.

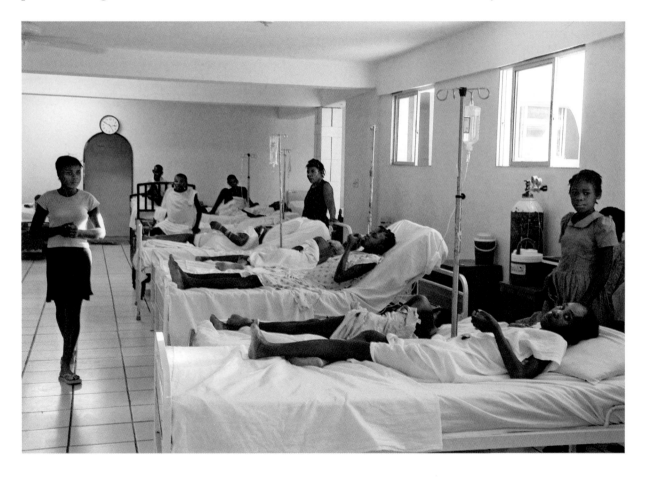

Population of Haiti's Largest Cities (2007 est.)

Port-au-Prince	1,321,522
Carrefour	482,123
Delmas	422,572
Cap-Haïtien	142,018
Pétionville	117,686

Children orphaned by HIV/AIDS line up outside a shelter.

Few Haitians talked publicly about HIV/AIDS until at least 1998. At that time, a woman named Esther Boucicault, whose husband and son had died of the disease, went on television to talk about it. Most people were scandalized that she would speak about HIV/AIDS in public, because the disease is often spread by sexual contact. Boucicault and others founded the National Solidarity Organization to help people with HIV/AIDS.

Because of both violence and AIDS, Haiti has the highest percentage of orphans of any country in the Western Hemisphere. The United Nations estimates that some 434,000 Haitian children are orphans. Port-au-Prince alone has an estimated 2,000 street children, most of them orphans.

These girls were rescued from their lives as restavecs.

Some children who have homes to live in are also in trouble. Children called *restavecs* are treated as slaves. *Restavecs* is a Creole term meaning "stay with." Desperately poor parents send their children, usually girls, to live with and work for other people. The parents do this in the hope that the children will get an education. In return, the families get cheap labor. This deal seldom does the children any good. Instead, they must work long hours, and they are often starved and beaten. Most do not get any education.

As Haiti becomes poorer, more and more children are being sent away to become restavecs. It's estimated that Haiti may have 300,000 child slaves.

Persons per square mile		Persons per square kilometer
260–517		100–200
130–259		50–99
65–129		25–49
25–64		10–24
3–24		1–9

More than a hundred thousand Haitians have sailed across the open sea hoping to reach Florida. Most make the long, dangerous journey in tiny wooden boats.

Where Have the People Gone?

Since the 1950s, millions of people have left Haiti. Most could no longer stand the violence and poverty. The first to leave were professionals, who moved away seeking better education and job opportunities. This flow of professionals out of Haiti increased under François Duvalier's oppression. In the 1960s, less skilled workers also began to leave. In one twenty-year period, the U.S. government issued visas (permits to enter the country) to more than a million Haitians.

A new wave of immigration began in 1972, when desperate Haitians began fleeing the country in small boats. They tried to sail the 700 miles (1,125 km) to South Florida, hoping to get onto land before U.S. government officials found them and sent them home. This group became known as the boat people.

It is estimated that 1.5 million people left Haiti during the early 1990s. Today, most of those emigrants live in the United States, Canada, and the Dominican Republic.

In recent years, Haiti has become more stable. Some Haitians living elsewhere have tried to return to Haiti. Some moved back. Others have gone home to visit friends and family. Today, the Haitian government is encouraging more Haitians living abroad to invest in their traditional home.

Desperate Waters

During the winter of 1991–92, many Haitians who had supported Jean-Bertrand Aristide feared for their lives and the future. The military had ousted Aristide, and now they were killing his supporters. The Duvalier years had destroyed the country's economy, and many Haitians were unable to support themselves.

During that one winter, more than forty thousand people tried to get from Haiti to southern Florida in whatever boat they could find. Those who survived the seas were usually caught by the U.S. Coast Guard and taken to a U.S. naval base. Those who could prove they were in genuine danger because of their political activity were allowed into the United States. Only a few qualified. Those who seemed to be seeking relief from poverty were returned to Haiti.

This policy drew criticism from other nations. In 1999, new immigration rules made it possible for Haitians who were in the United States illegally to apply for legal status.

Spiritual Life

THE SLAVES BROUGHT TO HAITI FROM AFRICA HAD strong religious beliefs. In Haiti, the slaves' African traditions merged with the teachings of Roman Catholicism, which was practiced by the Spanish and French. This merger created a new religion. Often called "Voodoo" in the United States, its accurate name is Vodou. The term comes from West Africa, where it means "spirit." Most Haitians consider themselves Roman Catholic, but they also believe the Vodou spirits are important in their lives.

Opposite: **Christianity and Vodou mix in Haiti**

Haiti's largest pilgrimage takes place on Good Friday. Catholic and Vodou faithful climb a steep path, praying at crosses along the way.

Ideas About Zombis

Some Vodou followers believe that a person's soul can be stolen by black magic. The person without a soul is a *zombi*, or undead person, who is then under the control of the magician.

Some scientists think that the idea of zombis began long ago, when priests gave people drugs that produced trances. Wade Davis, a scientist who supports this theory, wrote a book called *The Serpent and the Rainbow*. In 1988, a popular horror film was made from the book.

For many Haitians, the zombi is a metaphor for slavery. It is a state that must be refused and avoided.

taken over by a lwa. The person is then thought to be speaking for that particular god. Priests also control the use of herbs and medicines.

In Vodou, birds are sacrificed so their blood can be "fed" to the lwa, making the spirits stronger.

The spirits of a person's ancestors also are lwa. They need to be honored through Vodou rituals. These include prayer, dancing, drumming, and animal sacrifice. Because ancestors are so important, elaborate tombs are often built for the dead.

Animal sacrifice has always been a part of Vodou. Generally, a small animal such as a sheep or chicken will have its throat cut during the ritual. Some of the blood is usually collected and used in the ceremony. After the ceremony, the animal is cooked and eaten so that no scarce food is wasted.

Musicians play tubes called *vaksins* at a Vodou Easter ceremony.

Celebrating Rara

In the Christian calendar, the forty days before Easter is a period called Lent. During those days, Christians are supposed to lead quiet lives thinking about Christ's death. Many countries have huge celebrations, called Carnival, in the last days before Lent begins.

In Haiti, Carnival is called Rara. All over the country, friends and neighbors put together Rara bands and parade through the countryside. The band members often dance, do magic tricks, and chant as they move. The Artibonite Valley in central Haiti and the town of Léogâne, to the west of Port-au-Prince, are known for their colorful Rara bands. The band members usually wear bright clothing, often decorated with beads and sequins.

Haiti's Religions

Roman Catholic	80%
Protestant	16%
None	1%
Other	3%

Note: Most Roman Catholics also practice Vodou.

Spiritual Life **97**

Rara song lyrics often deal with issues of politics and poverty. Rara bands have sometimes been banned because of their political comments.

Other Faiths

For most of Haiti's history, the country's official religion has been Roman Catholicism. The Catholic faith was brought to the island by the Spanish and reinforced by the French.

Catholicism has been the dominant religion in Haiti since Spanish explorers first arrived there five hundred years ago.

Today, about 80 percent of Haitians call themselves Roman Catholic, though many also practice Vodou. The Roman Catholic Church has often officially condemned Vodou but in fact generally tolerates it.

About 16 percent of Haitians are Protestant. One of the first Protestant groups to gain a foothold in Haiti was the Baptist Church. Many Haitians went to Cuba to work in the

About 10 percent of Haitians belong to the Baptist Church, the nation's largest Protestant group. Another 4 percent are Pentecostal.

Blending Religions

Hundreds of years ago, slaves in Haiti began associating saints and other Catholic holy figures with the various lwa of Vodou. Catholic Saint Peter, for example, is called Papa Legba in Vodou. He is thought to control entry into the spirit world, just as Saint Peter is said to control entry of humans into Heaven. Sometimes pictures of saints are placed on the altars of Vodou temples.

1930s. Some brought their new Baptist beliefs back with them. The Baptist Church has since grown and spread throughout Haiti. The number of Evangelical Protestants has been rising rapidly in recent years. These groups teach a strict code of behavior and believe that the Bible is the final authority. Evangelicals strongly condemn Vodou. They say it is superstition and perhaps controlled by the Devil.

Some of the slaves brought to Haiti were Muslim, followers of the religion of Islam. Islam probably came close to dying out among the slaves in Haiti, but it was reintroduced to the country in the twentieth century by immigrants. Today, the country is home to a few thousand Muslims. The nation's first mosque, or Muslim house of worship, opened in 1985.

Haiti's Religious Holidays

Carnival	February or March
Holy Thursday	March or April
Good Friday	March or April
Easter Sunday	March or April
Assumption Day	August 15
All Saints' Day	November 1
All Souls' Day	November 2
Christmas	December 25

Patron Saints

In Haiti, each town has a patron saint, a Catholic holy person whose life the town celebrates with festivals. For example, the city of Lascahobas celebrates St. Benoit on March 21. The entire nation celebrates Mary, the mother of Jesus, on June 27. As Haiti's patron saint, she is called Our Lady of Perpetual Help.

Tradition holds that Christopher Columbus's interpreter was Jewish. Over time, some Jewish businessmen came to Haiti to work for French companies. Some were later forced to leave, and many were killed in the Haitian Revolution. Some Jewish immigrants from the Middle East began to arrive in Haiti a hundred years ago. Haiti's Jewish population has probably never been more than a few hundred. Most Jews live in Port-au-Prince.

A leader of Haiti's tiny Jewish community holds the only Torah scroll in Haiti. The Torah is the holiest book in Judaism.

Sights and Sounds

From its founding, Haiti has been a mix of African and French cultural influences that it melded into its own unique rhythms. Haitian culture generally developed in isolation, making it different from that of other Caribbean islands. Much of the distinctive art and music grows out of Vodou.

Opposite: **Drums and horns are central to Haitian music.**

Albert Mangonès made the Monument to the Unknown Maroon in 1968.

From Drums to Roots

Music has played a large role in Haitian culture. During rebellions, Haitian slaves communicated using the beat of drums and the trumpeting sound of big shells called conchs. The figure in the Monument to the Unknown Maroon is shown blowing on a conch shell to start the slave rebellion of 1791.

In the Haitian countryside, people have long made their own musical instruments. The *vaksin* is a hollow bamboo tube that makes a single sound. The size of the tube determines the sound, so several tubes of different length are put together as a single instrument. The largest (and thus deepest) is called the *manman*.

The Vodou Drums

The most famous Haitian drum is the *tanbou*. These tall, round drums originated in West Africa. Many rhythms used in Haitian music require that three of these drums be played at once. Both Rara bands and Vodou ceremonies feature tanbou drums.

Popular drummer Gaston Jean-Baptiste makes his own drums using methods passed down for hundreds of years. He is also a Vodou priest, and he drums to summon the lwa.

The smallest is the *tipeti*. Similarly, trumpets called *konè* are pounded out of sheet metal. They, too, make only one sound each. Individuals must work together to produce music.

Simple homemade instruments are a tradition in rural Haiti.

Much of today's music is called *mizik rasin*, "roots music." A combination of Vodou ritual music, traditional Haitian folk music, and rock 'n' roll, mizik rasin began in the late 1970s with the Vodou rock band Boukman Eksperyans. The group's founder, Lolo Beaubrun, was not raised in the Vodou religion, so he had to study Vodou in order to incorporate its rhythms into his music.

Singer Emerante de Pradine was the first Haitian woman to sign a record deal. She performs traditional Vodou songs. Her son, Richard Morse, leads a Vodou-style rock group called RAM. Morse grew up in the United States but now lives in Port-au-Prince.

RAM uses Rara horns and other traditional instruments in their music. Their songs have lyrics in Creole, French, and English.

Another type of Haitian music is called *twoubadou*. The term comes from the French word *troubadour*, a kind of folksinger. Twoubadou singers usually perform to the accompaniment of acoustic guitars. The music is a combination of Cuban songs that Haitian sugar plantation workers brought back home in the 1920s and merengue, a Latin music style that spread throughout Hispaniola. Ti-Coca, one of Haiti's greatest singers, has been performing twoubadou for more than thirty years.

The Queen of Haitian Song

Singer and songwriter Emeline Michel is sometimes called the Queen of Haitian Song. Michel is beloved for her mesmerizing voice and often political lyrics. Her music is notable for combining traditional Haitian rhythms with jazz or Latin music.

Michel was born in Gonaïves. At eighteen, she won a contest to study jazz in Detroit, Michigan, for a year. She returned to Haiti, where she built her career, and has since lived in France, Canada, and now New York. "Living outside of your own country, it's easy to sometimes feel that you have let your country down," she has said. "Everybody knows that Haiti is in trouble. Sometimes I feel like I should be there helping!" To Michel, making music is a way of helping. "It's my chance to show a side of Haitian culture that is positive."

From Music to Charity

Wyclef Jean is a Grammy Award–winning musician who is determined to improve life for his fellow Haitians. Jean was born in Croix-des-Bouquets in 1972. His family moved to New York City when he was nine and then settled in New Jersey. As a young man, he became famous as part of a hip-hop group called the Fugees. When he went solo and began doing his own writing, he turned to more traditional Haitian music. He also began recording in Creole. Jean wrote the music for the film *The Agronomist*, a documentary about Jean Dominique, a Haitian activist who was murdered.

In the wake of his own success, Jean founded a charity called Yéle Haiti. The group gives scholarships and works with other organizations involved in improving Haiti's health-care system and environment. Because of Jean's tireless work on behalf of his native country, in 2007 the Haitian government named him Haiti's roving ambassador to the world. As ambassador, he will promote the country's image abroad and encourage development.

Tap-taps are covered with color and often words. Each tap-tap has a name, which is sometimes painted on the front.

Artists

Haitian art is often brilliantly colored and boldly exuberant. Some of the most amazing art is seen on tap-taps, the odd assortment of vehicles used as buses. The tap-taps are elaborately painted. Many are painted fresh each year by a different artist.

In 1944, Port-au-Prince's Centre d'Art was established by an American teacher, Dewitt Peters, and Haitian artist Albert Mangonès (1917–2002) to encourage local artists. The work of Wilson Bigaud and Enguerrand Gourgue was among the results. Many of the center's artists achieved a primitive look, sometimes called naïve painting, which they used to show Haitian history and religious themes. Philome Obin (1891–1986) was a great painter of historical scenes. His work can be found in art museums around the world.

Philome Obin painted these murals at the Holy Trinity Cathedral.

In the 1950s, many artists involved in the center made paintings for the Holy Trinity Cathedral at Port-au-Prince. The church is decorated with spectacular murals by Obin, Bigaud, and others. The murals show religious themes in Haitian style. Many people consider the cathedral one of the highlights of Port-au-Prince.

Haitian artists use whatever they have, however they can, to create their work. The small town of Croix-des-Bouquet is known for its metal sculptures. The items look as if they were made of expensive wrought iron, but they are really made from oil drums. Among the city's great sculptors are Serge Jolimeau and Damien Paul.

Priest and Artist

Hector Hyppolite (1894–1948) was involved with the Centre d'Art in its early days. Before that, he was a Vodou priest. After Hyppolite made a journey to Africa, he felt that his lwa called him to paint his beliefs. He completed more than 150 works using his fingers and chicken feathers instead of paintbrushes.

Hyppolite's colors are vivid and clashing; the details, often smudged. His paintings mix Vodou and Roman Catholic images, demonstrating the Haitian blend of Christianity and African beliefs.

Writers Past and Present

Throughout Haitian history, writers have gotten into trouble with the people in power. Many Haitian writers have been forced to leave the country so that they can write freely.

Antoine Dupré, who was born in 1782, is generally considered Haiti's first writer. Dupré, who fought in the revolution, wrote both poetry and plays. His "Hymn to Liberty" is still quoted today. He was killed in a duel in 1816.

The Ardouin family produced several writers. In the 1830s, historian Beaubrun Ardouin wrote the first Haitian textbook, which dealt with the country's geography. He later wrote an eleven-volume history of Haiti that is still a major reference work on the early years of the country. His younger brother, Cariolan, was a talented poet, though his poems were not published until after his death at the age of twenty-four.

Jacques Stephen Alexis worked to foster a literary world in Haiti. He published his first novel, *General Sun, My Brother*, in 1955. It concerns the trials of a poor farmworker. Alexis became involved in politics and was forced to leave Haiti. When he returned in 1961, he was captured by the Tonton Macoutes and killed.

The best-known female novelist of the Duvalier period was Marie Chauvet. Though she had been writing novels since the 1950s, her 1968 book *Amour, Colère et Folie* brought her the most critical acclaim. Because it dealt with the evils of the Duvalier regime, all copies in Haiti were destroyed and it is still hard to come by. It has never been translated into English.

Edwidge Danticat's novels often concern Haitian history. One deals with the Taino ruler Anacaona, while another centers on a torturer in the Duvalier era.

The most famous Haitian writer today is Edwidge Danticat, who was born in Port-au-Prince in 1969. Danticat moved to New York when she was twelve. By then, she had acquired a deep love of her homeland and of Haitian storytelling. Though she did not learn English until she moved to New York, she was soon writing short stories in that language.

When a Haitian is ready to tell a story, he or she asks, Krik? The listeners answer excitedly, Krak! This exuberant practice provided the title of Danticat's first story collection, *Krik? Krak!* Her 1998 novel *The Farming of Bones* won the American Book Award.

Films and Filmmakers

Prize-winning filmmaker Raoul Peck was born in Port-au-Prince in 1953. His family fled the Duvalier dictatorship, and he was raised in Africa, in the Republic of Congo. Peck studied filmmaking in Germany and then began making movies in 1984. He returned to Haiti as minister of culture after democracy was restored, but he resigned eighteen months later.

Peck's films have won awards the world over. His movie *Sometimes in April* concerns the relationship between two brothers set against the backdrop of terrible violence in the African nation of Rwanda. Peck lives primarily in the United States, but he also has a small farm in Haiti.

Writer Dany Laferrière was born in Port-au-Prince in 1953. He left the country after a good friend was murdered in 1976. Laferrière settled in Canada, where he began writing short stories, novels, and films. His films include *Voodoo Taxi* and *Heading South*.

Sports

Soccer is the most popular team sport in Haiti, as it is in most of the world. Every four years, the top national teams from around the world compete in the World Cup. It is the world's most-watched sporting event. Haiti qualified for the World Cup for the first time in 1974. Never before had a team from a Caribbean island qualified.

Today, Haiti boasts both men's and women's national soccer teams. Soccer is hugely popular among children. They play pickup games in the streets and fields throughout the country.

One of Haiti's earliest sports heroes was Sylvio Cator. In the 1928 Olympics, Cator came in second in the long jump, earning a silver medal. That same year, he set a world record in the long jump, leaping 26 feet ¼ inch. Never before had a human being jumped more than 26 feet!

Basketball is also popular in Haiti. Though Haiti has its own basketball league, many of the best players move to the United States to play. Jobin Pascal moved to Canada, where he is now head coach of the Quebec City team.

Many people enjoy getting out into Haiti's warm, shallow waters. The chance to see marine life among the coral makes snorkeling popular with visitors. Many Haitians like to fish. They head out into the water to catch grouper, tuna, marlin, and bonito.

Mesidor Louivena of the Haitian national soccer team battles for the ball in a game against Cuba.

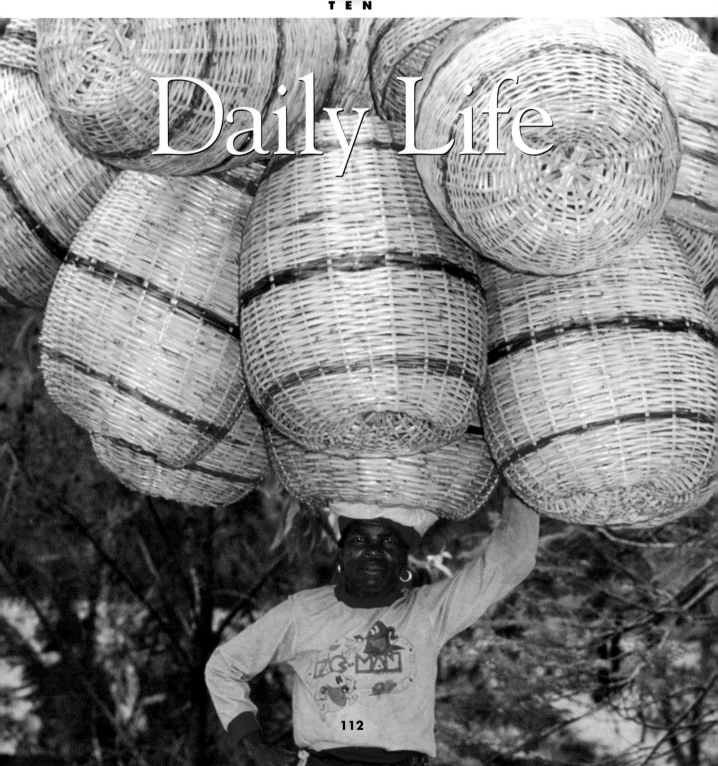

Daily Life

I
N MANY WAYS, HAITI IS LIKE OTHER ISLANDS IN THE Caribbean. Its people are fortunate to have lots of sunshine, beautiful oceans, good seafood, colorful art, and lively music. But Haitians also face desperate poverty and violence. Everyday life can be a struggle.

Opposite: **A woman carries homemade baskets to sell at a market.**

Celebrating the Holidays

Haiti celebrates many holidays throughout the year. Some holidays recall important dates in Haitian history. Battle of Vertières Day celebrates the Haitian victory over the French in the final battle of the Haitian Revolution. Other public holidays are rooted in religion. November 1 is All Saints' Day,

Marching bands take to the streets during Carnival.

a day that honors Christian holy people. The next day is All Souls' Day, which is sometimes called the Day of the Dead. It is an important holiday dedicated to remembering ancestors. Traditionally, people wore only white or gray on All Souls' Day. Vodou rituals are held in cemeteries on All Souls' Day. People pay particular attention to Baron Samedi, the lwa of the dead.

As part of the Christmas celebration, Haitian children often make *fanals*. These are cardboard churches with pretend stained-glass windows. Inside, a candle or small lamp shines.

Skulls adorn a Vodou temple. Vodou rituals abound in cemeteries and temples on All Souls' Day.

National Holidays

January 1	Independence Day
January 2	Ancestors' Day (also called Heroes' Day)
April 14	Pan-American Day
May 1	Labor and Agriculture Day
May 18	Flag and University Day
October 17	Anniversary of Dessalines's Death
October 24	United Nations Day
November 1	All Saints' Day
November 2	All Souls' Day
November 18	Battle of Vertières Day
December 5	Discovery of Haiti Day
December 25	Christmas Day

Haitians say that good children are visited by Santa Claus, who is called Ton-Ton Noël. Bad children are visited by Père Fouettard, who gives their parents a whip. No one knows what he looks like.

Both January 1 and January 2 are holidays. Some villages celebrate them by putting up a greased pole. Young men try to climb up to get a prize at the top. Most slide back down before can reach their prize.

Food

Many Haitian foods originated in Africa. Others have French or Spanish roots. Street vendors in cities sell snacks called *fritay*. One of the most popular fritay is *griyo*, a mixture of pork soaked in sour orange juice, hot peppers, and, sometimes, sweet potatoes.

Women selling grains, beans, and dried herbs at a market in Port-au-Prince

Rice and beans are a mainstay of the Haitian diet. Haitians also eat plenty of fruit, along with nuts and corn. People in the country rarely eat meat. Millet, a nutritious grain, is a common food among rural people.

Many Haitians do not get enough food. Hunger is often a daily fact of life. To combat hunger, organizations bring in food, especially for women and children. Violence, however, sometimes prevents workers from distributing food to those who need it.

Red Beans and Rice

Here's an easy recipe for delicious rice and beans.

Ingredients

1 cup dark-red kidney beans (dry, not canned)

4 cups water

¼ cup small cubes of bacon

2 tablespoons vegetable oil

1 cup chopped onion

2 cloves chopped garlic

1 cup chopped green pepper

2 cups cooked white rice

Salt and pepper to taste

Directions

Soak the beans in water overnight. Drain and rinse the beans. Put 4 cups of water in a medium-sized pot with the kidney beans. Bring the water to a boil. Turn down the heat until the water is just simmering. Cook for 2 hours, until the beans are tender. Drain the water into another container because you'll use it again.

In a heavy pot, fry the bacon cubes in vegetable oil until they are crisp.

Add the chopped onion, garlic, and green pepper to the frying pan, and stir the bacon-vegetable mixture often as it cooks. When the vegetables are tender, add the beans and the cooking water you put aside.

Bring the mixture to a boil again and add the rice. Reduce heat to a simmer. Cook for 15 to 20 minutes. Season with salt and pepper to taste.

Going to School

Haitians know that education is what will help pull them out of the mire of poverty. Throughout their history, however, schools have suffered from bad government and poverty. Violence has also sometimes kept teachers from showing up for work. As a result, many adult Haitians have a limited education. Less than one-quarter of Haitian families are headed by someone with more than a sixth-grade education; only about half the population can read and write.

Today, less than 15 percent of children under the age of eleven are enrolled in school. Most Haitian schools are run by churches. Because the teachers must be paid, even poor families must pay tuition of up to US$100 per child per year, plus the cost of uniforms and books. The average Haitian family spends a greater part of its income on education than families do in any other country in the world. The number of public schools has been shrinking for years. President René Préval is looking for help from foreign organizations to achieve his goal of universal grade-school education by 2015.

After age eleven, students whose families can afford it go on to secondary school, which lasts for seven years. Those students are much more likely to be boys than girls. In Haiti, secondary schools are usually called colleges. One of the oldest and most elite secondary schools is Collège St. Louis de Gonzague in Port-au-Prince.

Schoolchildren in Haiti are required to wear uniforms. Some children cannot go to school because their families can't afford the uniforms.

Only 2 percent of Haitian children finish secondary school. Very few go to university. Higher education is free at Haiti State University. The university has about ten thousand students, but it has few full-time professors. Two new universities were founded recently, both in Port-au-Prince. The University of Caraibe was founded in 1988, and the University Notre Dame of Haiti in 1995. Caraibe also has a small campus in Montrouis-Cadenette. Some Protestant groups have also started university-level schools.

Perhaps 3 to 5 percent of Haitians are rich. They live in lavish homes, sometimes with swimming pools.

The Rich and the Rest

Wealthy people in Haiti's cities carry on their lives as people do all around the world. They go to work and enjoy their free time. They dine out in restaurants and shop in fine stores. Some even have servants in their homes.

Life is quite different for the vast majority of Haitians, however. Many people in Haiti do not have regular jobs. Instead they work as farmers, market sellers, or at other temporary jobs. Much of the time, they are without work.

Cockfighting is hugely popular among Haitian men. Virtually no women attend the fights.

Their days are filled with other activities. People who practice Vodou often spend a great deal of time dealing with the lwa. Some men put a lot of effort into cockfighting. They devote a lot of time and money to preparing their roosters to fight. The roosters have sharp spurs attached to their feet, which they use to gouge their opponents. The losing cock usually dies. The men watching the cockfight bet on which rooster will win.

Housing

In Port-au-Prince, many buildings, especially hotels, are sparkling white and ornate, like fancy birthday cakes. Older city houses are often trimmed the same way, with woodwork curlicues called gingerbread.

Smaller houses are usually white with brightly colored trim. Most of the urban houses built in recent years are made of concrete blocks and have tin roofs. They generally have shutters on the windows that can be closed to keep out the hot noonday sun.

Because of crowding around the cities, more houses are being built on the neighboring mountainsides. With few trees to keep the soil in place around them, however, these houses sometimes slide away when it rains.

Slum Life

Much of Port-au-Prince is now a slum. Shantytowns, with houses made of cardboard or tin, have grown, house by house, up the hillsides and out onto the beaches. Life in these slums

More than fifty slums surround Port-au-Prince. More people live in these slums than in the city itself.

is bleak and often violent. Most people in the slums are young and have nothing to do.

The country's largest slum is Cité Soleil. It is the worst section of Port-au-Prince. Some would say it is the worst section of the entire Western Hemisphere. Violent gangs came to dominate Cité Soleil in the 1990s. These gangs used children as messengers and spies. They gave children weapons to use to prevent outsiders from entering Cité Soleil. For years, the gangs even kept out aid workers who were trying to bring in food and other supplies.

Immediately after René Préval was elected president in 2006, aid workers entered Cité Soleil to reopen schools, make water available, and provide some health services. Gangs agreed to give up their weapons. Even in Cité Soleil, there is a glimmer of hope.

A Way Ahead in the Slums

L'Athletique d'Haiti ("Athletes of Haiti") is an organization in Cité Soleil and other slums dedicated to giving kids a chance to practice soccer and to have a hot meal. The children—almost six hundred of them—must attend school to be in the program. The program was started by former soccer star Bobby Duval, who spent time in prison for opposing François Duvalier. The organization is now supported by Wyclef Jean's charity, Yéle Haiti. Duval also hopes to break down class barriers in Haiti by having his team of kids from the slums play against teams of wealthier children.

A woman stands in front of her mud house in rural Haiti. In houses like this, the kitchen is outside.

Life in Rural Areas

In many countries, people who are unable to make a living in rural areas move to the city. Though some Haitians do that, many know that life is no better in the cities. Also, many own at least a small bit of land.

In rural areas, houses tend to be small. They are often made of mud molded onto sticks and then dried in the sun. Some houses are also made of bamboo. Roofs are usually made of grasses and sticks.

Few buildings in the countryside have electricity. Some communities may have a radio or a television that people share. Neighbors in rural areas are also likely to share big jobs, such as putting up a new building, harvesting a crop, or performing Vodou rituals.

Some people in the country use stems, vines, bark, and leaves to make baskets. Many Haitian families keep most of their possessions in baskets. Most Haitians carry loads on their heads, usually in baskets, instead of in their arms. Children learn this skill early.

Water and Sanitation

In both rural and urban areas, slightly less than half the population has access to drinkable water. Only about one-fourth of the people in rural areas have easy access to toilets; in cities, around half do.

Throughout the country, rivers and streams often carry human waste. Such pollution has serious health effects. Haiti suffers frequent outbreaks of typhoid, a sometimes deadly disease caused by drinking dirty water.

Scientists working in connection with Albert Schweitzer Hospital in Deschapelles have designed sand filters that can be used in homes to provide clean drinking water. The system was tested in the Artibonite Valley and will probably be used throughout the world in places where water is not safe.

Medical Care

Health care in Haiti is a mixture of Western medicine and Vodou ritual. Many Haitians first turn to Vodou priests for help when they are ill. The Haitian government offers little help for medical care, but the need is huge. More than 10 percent of Haitian children die before age five. An average Haitian can expect to live only fifty-two years.

Haitians have a choice of doctors in Port-au-Prince, but few doctors work in rural areas. Those who do are likely to be visiting doctors working for international organizations. The Albert Schweitzer Hospital was founded in 1956 by Larimer and Gwen Mellon of Arizona. At that time, there were no doctors in the Artibonite Valley, which was home to almost two hundred thousand people. The hospital has served as the main source of health care in the valley ever since.

A baby girl is given a vaccine. In 2005, only 43 percent of one-year-olds had received the vaccine for polio, a disease that can paralyze its victims.

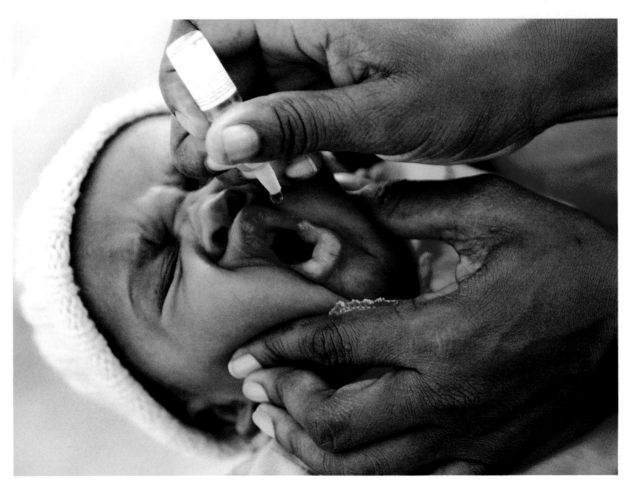

Partners in Health

Paul Farmer, an American doctor who is a professor at Harvard University in Massachusetts, cofounded an organization called Partners in Health in 1987. The group has proved that it is possible to effectively treat serious health problems in poor countries. They provide wide-ranging general care (above) and work in close partnership with people in the community.

Partners in Health traces its origins back to a small clinic that Farmer opened in the village of Cange, in central Haiti. The people of Cange had been pushed off their farms by the construction of a dam, and they were desperately poor.

As AIDS spread in Haiti, Farmer's group was at the center of the effort to identify and treat the disease all around the country. Rural people who suffer from HIV/AIDS have a hard time growing their own food. To deal with this, Haitians formed their own partner organization called Zanmi Lasante, which distributes food to HIV/AIDS patients. The Partners in Health system promotes hiring a family member or friend to make sure that the sick person takes the necessary AIDS drugs on schedule. Today, Farmer's way of working to improve health and social justice is being copied in other poor areas of the world.

Aid organizations also make sure that as many Haitian children as possible are given vaccines to prevent them from getting deadly diseases. Polio and measles have been eliminated from Haiti, but many other diseases remain serious problems.

Less Poverty, More Hope

President-elect René Préval said after the election of 2006, "Though ravaged, Haiti is not the wretched land as so often described in the media. It is a land of hope for more than eight million people. I cannot achieve miracles, nor have I been promising any. But I feel I have the responsibility to the Haitian people to open doorways on a brighter future: less poverty, less inequality, more wealth, more hope."

Haitians continue to hope, because, as one of their own sayings reminds them: "As long as the head is not cut off, the hope of wearing a hat remains."

A father and son sell flowers in Cité Soleil, perhaps the most dangerous area of Haiti.

Timeline

People first move to Hispaniola from **ca. 4000** B.C.
Central America.

Christopher Columbus lands on Hispaniola.   A.D. **1492**

Black Africans are first brought to   **1503**
Hispaniola.

The first French settlers arrive on   **1625**
Hispaniola.

The Treaty of Ryswick splits Hispaniola   **1697**
between France and Spain.

Port-au-Prince is founded as the capital   **1749**
of Haiti.

A slave uprising begins.   **1791**
Slavery is abolished in all French colonies.   **1794**

World History

2500 B.C.   Egyptians build the pyramids
and the Sphinx in Giza.

563 B.C.   The Buddha is born in India.

A.D.
313   The Roman emperor Constantine
legalizes Christianity.

610   The Prophet Muhammad begins preaching
a new religion called Islam.

1054   The Eastern (Orthodox) and Western
(Roman Catholic) Churches break apart.

1095   The Crusades begin.

1215   King John seals the Magna Carta.

1300s   The Renaissance begins in Italy.

1347   The plague sweeps through Europe.

1453   Ottoman Turks capture Constantinople,
conquering the Byzantine Empire.

1492   Columbus arrives in North America.

1500s   Reformers break away from the Catholic
Church, and Protestantism is born.

1776   The U.S. Declaration of Independence
is signed.

1789   The French Revolution begins.

Haitian History

Haiti achieves independence from France.	1804
Haiti gains control of Santo Domingo (now the Dominican Republic).	1822
The Dominican Republic becomes independent.	1844
The United States invades Haiti.	1915
U.S. troops are withdrawn from Haiti.	1934
The Dominican military murders thousands of Haitians along the Haitian border.	1937
François "Papa Doc" Duvalier becomes president.	1957
Duvalier dies; his son Jean-Claude "Baby Doc" Duvalier takes over.	1971
Jean-Claude Duvalier flees Haiti.	1986
Jean-Bertrand Aristide becomes president and is soon overthrown by the military.	1991
The military government is forced out; Aristide returns.	1994
Aristide is again elected president.	2000
René Préval is elected president.	2006

World History

1865	The American Civil War ends.
1879	The first practical light bulb is invented.
1914	World War I begins.
1917	The Bolshevik Revolution brings communism to Russia.
1929	A worldwide economic depression begins.
1939	World War II begins.
1945	World War II ends.
1957	The Vietnam War begins.
1969	Humans land on the Moon.
1975	The Vietnam War ends.
1989	The Berlin Wall is torn down as communism crumbles in Eastern Europe.
1991	The Soviet Union breaks into separate states.
2001	Terrorists attack the World Trade Center in New York City and the Pentagon in Washington, D.C.

Fast Facts

Official name: Republic of Haiti

Capital: Port-au-Prince

Official languages: French and Creole

Pétionville

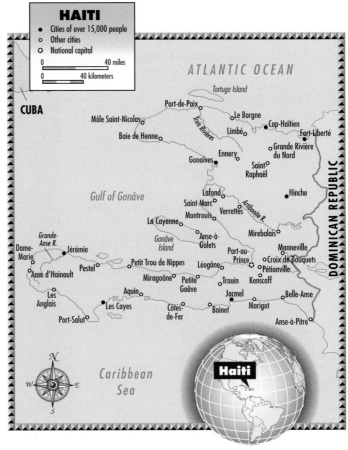

Haiti's flag

Saut d'Eau

Official religion:	None
Year of founding:	1804
National anthem:	"La Dessalinienne" ("Song of Dessalines")
Government:	Republic, but often taken over by military dictatorships
Chief of state:	President
Head of government:	Prime minister
Area:	10,714 square miles (27,750 sq km)
Borders:	Haiti's only land border is with the Dominican Republic.
Coastline:	1,131 miles (1,820 km) long
Highest elevation:	Pic la Selle, 8,793 feet (2,680 m) above sea level
Lowest elevation:	Sea level, along the coast
Average temperature:	75°F (24°C) in January and 83°F (28°C) in July, with higher elevations about 10°F (5°C) cooler
Average annual rainfall:	Varies from 5 inches (13 cm) in the northwest to more than 145 inches (360 cm) in the southwest
National population:	8,301,478 (2006 est.)

The Citadelle

Currency

Population of largest cities (2007 est.):

Port-au-Prince	1,321,522
Carrefour	482,123
Delmas	422,572
Cap-Haïtien	142,018
Pétionville	117,686

Famous landmarks:
- ▶ *The Citadelle,* Milot
- ▶ *Holy Trinity Cathedral,* Port-au-Prince
- ▶ *Pic Macaya National Park,* Massif de la Hotte
- ▶ *San Souci,* Milot
- ▶ *La Visite National Park,* Seguin

Industry: About two-thirds of Haitians work in agriculture, most growing barely enough to feed their families. The main agricultural exports are coffee, mangoes, cacao, and rice. About 9 percent of the labor force works in industry, primarily sugar refining, textiles, and light manufacturing. Unemployment in Haiti is high. More than two-thirds of adults are unemployed or do not have regular jobs.

Currency: The gourde, which is divided into 100 centimes. In 2007, US$1 equaled 39 gourdes, and 1 gourde equaled about 2 ½ U.S. cents.

System of weights and measures: Haiti officially uses the metric system, but the U.S. system is also used.

Literacy (2005 est.): 51%

Haitian girls

Toussaint Louverture

Common Creole words and phrases:

Wi	Yes
Non	No
Mesi	Thank you
Souple	Please
Prese prese!	Hurry!
Jodia	Today
Konben?	How much?

Famous Haitians:

Anacaona *Taino queen*	(1474–1503)
Jean-Bertrand Aristide *Former president*	(1953–)
Edwidge Danticat *Novelist*	(1969–)
Jean-Jacques Dessalines *Leader of the slave revolt*	(ca. 1758–1806)
Jean Dominique *Murdered reporter and activist*	(1930–2000)
François Duvalier *Dictator*	(1907–1971)
Hector Hyppolite *Artist*	(1894–1948)
Wyclef Jean *Musician*	(1972–)
Félix Morisseau-Leroy *Writer*	(1912–1998)
Toussaint Louverture *Leader of the slave revolt*	(ca. 1743–1804)

To Find Out More

Books

▶ Goldstein, Margaret J. *Haiti in Pictures*. Minneapolis: Lerner, 2005.

▶ Kallen, Stuart A. *Voodoo*. San Diego: Lucent Books, 2005.

▶ Myers, Walter Dean. *Toussaint L'ouverture: The Fight for Haiti's Freedom*. New York: Simon & Schuster, 1996.

▶ Temple, Bob. *Haiti*. Philadelphia: Mason Crest, 2004.

DVDs

▶ *True Caribbean Pirates*. The History Channel. A&E Home Video. 2006.

▶ *Voodoo Secrets*. The History Channel. A&E Home Video. 2005.

Web Sites

▶ **Background Note: Haiti**
www.state.gov/r/pa/ei/bgn/1982.htmp
A variety of information about Haiti from the U.S. Department of State.

▶ **Haiti & the U.S.A.**
www.haiti-usa.org
*A site devoted to the intertwining
of U.S. and Haitian history.*

▶ **The Haiti Support Group**
www.haitisupport.gn.apc.org/
*For a range of information, from
current news to biographies of famous
Haitians.*

▶ **Smithsonian Global Sound**
www.smithsonianglobalsound.org
*To hear samples of music from around
the world. Choose a country from the
home page.*

Embassies and Organizations

▶ **Embassy of the Republic of Haiti
in Canada**
130 Albert Street, Suite 1500
Ottawa, Ontario K1P 5G4
Canada
613-238-1628

▶ **Embassy of the Republic of Haiti
in the United States**
2311 Massachusetts Ave., N.W.
Washington, D.C. 20008
202-332-4090
www.haiti.org

Index

Page numbers in *italics* indicate illustrations.

Meet the Author

JEAN F. BLASHFIELD delights in learning fascinating things about places and the people who live in them. Sometimes she learns too much! When writing a book for young people, she's often as challenged by what to leave out of the book as what to put in it.

Jean Blashfield was born in Madison, Wisconsin, and grew up near Chicago, Illinois. She graduated from the University of Michigan and went to work for Children's Press. After developing the *Young People's Science Encyclopedia* for that company, she moved to London, England, to live. She spent three years there, during which time she wrote her first books for young people.

Since then, she has written more than 135 books, most of them for young people. Besides writing about interesting places, she also loves history and science. In fact, one of her advantages as a writer is that she becomes fascinated by every subject she investigates. She has created an encyclopedia of aviation and space, written popular books on murderers and

house plants, and had a lot of fun creating a book on women's exploits called *Hellraisers, Heroines, and Holy Women.* She also founded the Dungeons & Dragons fantasy book department, which is now part of the gaming company Wizards of the Coast. These days, she is again writing fantasy for the Paths of Doom series.

Jean lives in the Lake Geneva area of Wisconsin, with her husband, Wallace Black, a publisher, writer, and pilot. She has two grown children. She treasures her cats and her computers, though not always in that order. In addition to researching via her computers, she produces whole books on the computer—scanning pictures, creating layouts, and even developing the index. She is an avid Internet surfer, but she'll never give up her trips to the library.

Photo Credits

Photographs © 2008:

Alamy Images: 72 (Fabienne Fossez), 7 top, 19 (Robert Harding Picture Library Ltd.), 68 (Hemis), 96 (Roger Hutchings), 27 top (Andre Jenny)

AP/Wide World Photos: 60 (Andres Leighton), 126 (Daniel Morel)

Art Directors and TRIP Photo Library: 104 bottom (Ark Religion.com), 112, 120, 123 (Ask Images), 40 (Edward Parker/Ark Religion.com)

Art Resource, NY/Réunion des Musées Nationaux: 46

Chatoyer Arts & Media/John Sann: 106 top

Corbis Images: 25, 113 (Daniel Aguilar/ Reuters), 106 bottom (Mario Anzuoni/ Reuters), 43, 108 bottom (Archivo Iconografico, SA), 2, 18 (Tony Arruza), 57 (Orlando Barria/EFE/epa), 15 (Carlos Barría/Reuters), 12, 36 top, 48, 51 top, 53, 55, 56 top, 56 bottom, 133 bottom (Bettmann), cover, 6 cover (Richard Bickel), 110 (Marc Brasz), 51 bottom (Gianni Dagli Orti), 37 (Clive Druett/ Papilio), 7 bottom, 82 (Owen Franken), 9, 17 (Rick Friedman), 90 (Jacques Langevin), 27 bottom, 130 left (Jacques Langevin/Sygma), 58 (Benjamin Lowy), 92, 122 (Eduardo Munoz/Reuters), 8 (Carl & Ann Purcell), 118 (Jerome Sessini/In Visu), 64 top, 114 (Les Stone/ZUMA), 85 (David Turnley), 98, 127 (Peter Turnley), 10 (Della Zuana Pascal/Sygma), 13

Cursorius Photo & Video Library/Leo JR Boon: 35 top

D. Donne Bryant Stock Photography: 79, 132 bottom (John Cotter), 101 (Larry Luxner)

Getty Images: 59 (AFP), 81, 88, 93, 97, 121 (Thony Belizaire), 80 (James P. Blair), 91 (Yuri Cortez), 28 (De Agostini Picture Library), 33 (Wolcott Henry), 47 (MPI), 89 top, 133 top (Robert Nickelsberg/Time Life Pictures), 66 (Scott Olson), 31 (Stan Osolinski), 62 bottom (Joe Raedle), 65 (Chantal Regnault), 45 bottom (Rischgitz), 111 (Martin Rose), 99 (Roberto Schmidt), 29, 87 (Shaul Schwarz)

ImageState/Jean-Claude Coutausse/ RAPHO: 24, 131 bottom

Index Stock Imagery: 23 (Alyx Kellington), 84 (Steve Starr), 64 bottom (Travel Ink Photo Library)

JupiterImages/Hemera Technologies: 30

Landov, LLC/Eduardo Munoz/Reuters: 35 bottom

Lonely Planet Images: 116 (Andrew Marshall & Leanne Walker), 42, 132 top (Stephen Saks), 70, 77 (Eric L. Wheater)

MapQuest.com, Inc.: 62 top, 131 top

National Geographic Image Collection/ James P. Blair: 26, 41

Nature Picture Library Ltd./Solvin Zankl: 32

Panos Pictures: 103 (Jean-Leo Dugast), 78, 83 (Mark French)

Photo Researchers, Inc: 76 (Andy Crump/ TDR/WHO), 36 bottom (Jeff Lepore), 38 (Tom McHugh), 39 (N. Smythe)

Reuters/Eduardo Munoz: 125

Superstock, Inc.: 104 top (David Forbert), 61, 108 top

The Image Works: 75 (Mario Algaze), 102, 105 (ArenaPal/Topham), 95 (Tony Clark), 74 (Louise Gubb), 71 (Peter Hvizdak), 21 (Larry Mangino), 52 (Mary Evans Picture Library), 34 (John Moore), 119 (Jean-Yves Rabeuf), 107 (Tony Savino), 16 (Sean Sprague), 45 top (TIW Archives)

United States Geological Survey/Coastal and Marine Geology Program: 22

Maps by XNR Productions, Inc.